The Revolutionary Social Worker

The Love Ethic Model

Dyann Ross

IIR

REVOLUTIONARIES

Brisbane, Australia

ISBN 978-0-6487999-2-4

Cover artwork by Amanda Espinosa
Book design and typesetting by Paula Pomer

First published in 2020

Revolutionaries
Brisbane, Australia
www.revolutionaries.com.au

Contents

Chapter 2   29
The love ethic model in social work

Acknowledgements

I would like to acknowledge the Gubbi Gubbi People of the Sunshine Coast area of south east Queensland. I pay my respects to their Elders, past, present and emerging. Their stewardship of nature over thousands of years means I am living and working in an amazingly beautiful place.

As I finish this little book with big ideas to live by, I am keenly aware of the impact of COVID-19 across the world. I wish to acknowledge the people who are caring for others and who pay forward their love. I feel deeply saddened for the suffering and loss so many people and communities are experiencing, including from the flow-on economic and other impacts.

An acknowledgements page is not so easy to write as I want to thank everyone which doesn't really mean anything. I will for now acknowledge the person who has given me crucial support as I wrote the book and in getting it published. That person is Wallea Eaglehawk who has established an exciting publishing company for books about love as revolutionary. Revolutionaries is the perfect place to have my book published and that it is my daughter's creation makes it very special indeed.

Chapter 1
Values for revolutionary work

The book is an invitation to you, the reader, to position yourself as a citizen-cum-social worker to join up with me and expand social work's domains of concern and ways of practising. Chapter 1 begins by introducing the idea of the person as revolutionary. This idea is linked to social workers whose values and actions align with the love ethic model and love informed ethics work. An evocative poetic is presented to convey some of my biography which is intricately embedded in a lifetime of relationships and experiences. The chapter presents an overview of some problematics of violence, namely, domestic violence, child sexual abuse, professional privilege, animal violence and ecological violence. These are, in different ways, examples of interpersonal violence, lovelessness and injustice which constitute the domains of concern for the revolutionary social worker.

This sets the scene for introducing a range of values which are integral to social work and form the basis upon which the love ethic model was created. The love ethic model is needed to enable revolutionary social workers to address the problematics of violence. The adoption of an ecological imagination extends the domains of concern for social workers to include social work in relationships with human-to-human, human-to-nonhuman animal and human-to-nature.

Chapter 2 describes the love ethic model and gives some indications about how-to-do-love-ethic work. In Chapter 3 a set of interrelated scenarios are utilised to provide examples of love ethic work. Arising from these examples, the ethical and practice complexities are outlined. Chapter 4 offers a forward invitation for us to join with others to: hold a loving vision; foster active hope; support emerging signs of new ways; and, to uphold already known nonviolent and just ways that are working. It includes examples of loving ecological and posthuman steps, that is steps which de-centre human dominance and rationality. Steps such as learning the language of trees to build empathy with nonhuman species.

The Glossary provides working definitions of key concepts in the love ethic model.

There is a resource for the book called *The Revolutionary Social Worker: Love Ethic Companion* which offers an interpretation of ethical theories, ethico-legal principles and anti-discriminatory conventions and legislation which are consistent with the love ethic.

The person as revolutionary

A revolutionary is a nonviolent, loving and justice seeking citizen of the world. The book title could as readily be – the revolutionary citizen. However, the title - the revolutionary social worker - brings a particular focus of the book to the role social workers can play in modelling and enabling revolutionary change. The book shows how the practice of being a revolutionary can look in specific relationships and contexts, and from the 'inside' of a profession that has potentially revolutionary goals. While the focus is on social workers, the term is inclusive of any profession and any citizen who seeks to enact the love ethic.

Tiruneh defines revolution as a "popular uprising that transforms an existing socioeconomic and political order" (2014, p. 10). The term is used in the book to refer to the large-scale change in values from imperialism, militarism, capitalism and patriarchal values to post-colonialism, disarmament, postcapitalism and posthumanist values. Revolutionary ways cannot be confined to the occasional street march or a singular campaign that protests an injustice. Further, the large-scale change needs to be enacted by millions of people in all aspects of citizens' life and work because of the intersectionality of oppression (Watts, 2015). This interpretation of revolution is juxtaposed with the popular idea of revolution as violent uprisings which involve destruction, large-scale loss of life, chaos and collapse of societies (Moro, 2016, p. 2).

The book promotes the idea of a quiet revolution of little acts of love by everyday people at home, at work, in their communities, with animals and in the natural environment. For present purposes, when these little acts cohere with the love ethic model the momentum is more potent. This is because the love ethic informed citizen grasps the nature of, and holds the tension with, the causes of harm and injustice on the planet. The revolution needs to occur in millions of relationships and places and can take many forms. The revolution is one of values, process and relationships and consists of actions that create peaceful, loving homes, safe and just workplaces, sustainable landscapes and nonviolent interspecies relationships.

The book draws on a broad range of theories of social change including critical mass theory (Oliver, 2013). An interpretation of this theory suggests that the revolution will occur when a sufficient number of people cultivate love informed values and enact them as a conscious, coherent ethical practice in their lives as citizens. Social workers can contribute to the building of this mass movement which is already occurring across the planet. Contemporary examples are the #MeToo movement (Nicolaou & Smith, 2019), the range of climate change projects with activists such as Greta Thunberg (Sengupta, 2020) and animal rights activist groups, including People for Ethical Treatment of Animals, PETA (2020) and Animals Australia (2019).

The personal and professional is political

My commitment to a loving, anti-oppressive ethical positionality sets the frame for the book with the question - why is the love ethic needed? It is inspired by my childhood and social work experiences of interpersonal and interspecies violence, lovelessness and injustice. The famous feminist dictum - the personal is political (Stanley & Wise, 1983) - applies in this book. Individual experiences occur in a socio-economic, cultural and political context which intricately influences personal stories of violence, disadvantage and survival struggles. I have consciously and deliberately drawn on my own childhood and social work experiences to inform my self-making and work with others. Thus, the professional is also political. Mills' (1959) influential idea of the sociological imagination is related to the personal is political dictum. He explains that the sociological imagination enables personal troubles of individuals to be understood as public issues requiring societal responses (Mills, 1959). I adapt it to include loving, anti-oppressive and posthumanist values and marry it with Thomashow's understanding of the ecological imagination. Thomashow defines the ecological imagination as:

The ability to move seamlessly through space and time, to expand vision, to think creatively, to improvise and adapt, to directly apprehend what is otherwise overlooked, to cultivate empathy and wisdom, to internalize biological and cultural diversity, and then finally to ask the big important questions about meaning and purpose. (2014, n.p.)

This section aims to convey some dimensions of my politics and positionality in the form of a sociological poetic (Ellis & Flaherty, 1992) and personal narrative. The approach combines "the personal, the biographical with the political [and] the social [where] the tale being told should reflect back on, be entangled in, and critique this current historical moment and its discontents" (Denzin, 1997, p. 200). The narrative is not attempting to depict true events in every instance. Rather, the purpose is to evoke ethical sensibilities to invite the reader to ponder the harm caused by violence, lovelessness and injustice. The narrative reflects the overall focus of the book on interpersonal violence.

This writing technique is similar to Lather and Smithies' (1997) use of intertexts between main chapters of their book as a deconstructive space. I use it here to decentre my claims of certainty, rationality and expertness to unsettle my authoritative voice as the author of the book. The socio-poetic is framed around lyrics from a song by Midnight Oil, entitled *Blue Sky Mine* (Hirst, Moginie, Garrett, Rotsey & Stevens, 1990). The lyrics are shown in italics.

Biographies of interlinked violence

There'll be food on the table tonight
She partly fills the small aluminium pot
(Funny that, that's what my dad makes – aluminium
And here's my mum keeping his dinner hot with it)
with water, puts it on the only working hotplate
on low heat and places the pot-lid-covered meal on top
He will be late home from the pub

There'll be pay in your pocket tonight
My stomach gets tighter for her

The Revolutionary Social Worker

It's pay day. We are out of bread and milk
There's no meat for dad's dinner
If he comes home straight away
We can buy in food and eat tonight

My gut is wrenched out it is scrunched up and broken
The beer mostly deadens the pain for him
But increases it for us
My little brother guzzles the last of the already diluted milk in his bottle
He still cries and won't settle
I get him into bed with me and Tess

My life is lived no more than a token
Who'll strike the flint upon the stone and tell me why?
The pub is shut, but still no dad
The terror builds inside.
She waits up, knitting
The waiting goes on forever
At last the sound of the car in our drive
I cuddle up closer to Tommy and Tess in the too small bed
But it still feels cold

If I yell at night there's a reply of silence
The one-sided yelling starts
He bangs on the table and breaks it
It's been a bad day, the furnace tap went wrong
She'll be getting his dinner off the stove
The loud crash catapults me towards the bedroom door
Which mum shuts when she thinks there will be trouble
I am shaking so badly I can go no further

After a nerve-wracking moment
I hear my mother pleading with him

At least she is OK, for now
I wake with a start
All is quiet, but a light still seeps in under my door
I creep out
She sits in a shrivelled heap, staring as the TV flickers
I know what she is thinking –
The screen is no comfort I can't speak my sentence
They blew the lights at heaven's gates and I don't know why
Their bedroom is full of stale beer and cigarettes
The smell makes me puke but I swallow it down
And hide away the fear for another night

But if I work all day on the blue sky mine
(There'll be food on the table tonight)
Still I walk up and down on the blue sky mine
(There'll be pay in your pocket tonight)

"Shhhhhh! Your father is sleeping!"

I can't remember when I last saw him
He's either asleep, at work or at the pub
Or shooting kangaroos up the bush with his mates
Ron says he likes it that way
At least he is not getting belted for sticking up for mum
He helps dad gut and clean the carcasses
The blood from the animals stains the ground

The candy store paupers lie to the shareholders
They're crossing their fingers they pay the truth makers
The balance sheet is breaking up the sky
"No, you can't go! Ron, stop picking on him," screams mum
"Yeh, you big bully," interjects Sam
"Sam, you keep out of it! Ron! If you don't stop it, I'll tell your father on you!"

"But why, mum?" I continue on dangerous ground
"Because I said so!"
"But mum, all the other kids are going!"
"Don't back chat me young lady! What do you think I am – a money tree?"

My face stings from a sharp slap
I don't ask again
My brother gets to go on his school camp
She hides the unpaid bills
What dad doesn't know, doesn't hurt him
Her ulcer festers
She eats less so there is more to go round
The girls get smaller pieces of meat & sometimes none at all
"Why is there never enough?" mum wonders out loud

So I'm caught at the junction still warming for medicine
I go to the shop to get her Bex tablets
Mum's headaches have been real bad lately
Dad says she's going crazy!
Ron belts dad and tells him to shut his dirty rotten mouth
But Ron mostly is out in the shed, his hideout from trouble
Tess runs there when dad's late home
She says Ron treats her real nice
He hugs her all night

The sweat on my brow keeps on feeding the engine
Hope the crumbs in my pocket can keep me for another night
Ron has a job at the local abattoir
He is a boner
He helps with meat off cuts when he can
Ron and his mates drink a lot and joke
About how the sheep bleat and become panic-stricken
Even before they are unloaded from the truck

And if the blue sky mining company won't come to my rescue
If the sugar refining company won't save me
Who's gonna save me?

Childhood stolen
Years of angry outbursts and violence
Dad and Ron seem to take turns
In their warped brand of discipline
Ron is more like dad since he went to the abattoirs
He has nightmares too!
Tess helps him by spending more time in his shed
Mum keeps the house running
So much washing, cooking, bathing the littlies, cleaning
No end of it all
I wish I could save Tess, our family, the sheep, the kangaroos
But if I work all day on the blue sky mine

The mining company says there will be no job losses
Dad says they're bastards!
They are giving him a bad time 'cause he's the union rep
And some have sailed from a distant shore
And the company takes what the company wants

The strike is now into its 12th day
The Salvos brought a food parcel to the door
Mum wouldn't let me take it
The parcel even had chocolates in it!
I feel her shame and desperation
And nothing is as precious
as a hole in the ground

Who's gonna save me?
He returns to work

The Revolutionary Social Worker

I am glad he still has a job
I can't make it better
I feel guilty

I pray that sense and reason brings us in
The yelling and crashing happens more now
I beg God to stop the fighting
He doesn't hear me
Dad spreads his endless pain into all of us
We are bonded together in a deathly struggle
But not only us
The neighbour killed his two dogs in a fit of rage last night
I heard him bashing them with a metal pole
Missing sometimes and hitting the clothesline
His wife was begging him to stop
He then turned on her
The children ran out onto the street screaming

Who's going to save the children?
Who is going to save my mum?
Who is going to save our family?
Mum goes to counselling
She stops after two times
Swearing about their upitty ways and
Angry they are telling her to leave dad
She doesn't tell them of her time
At Lindsay Miller hospital when she got the shock treatment

We've got nothing to fear
Until he comes home
Until Ron moves onto my littlest sister
Who's going to save the animals?
I can still hear the dogs yelping

Until the neighbour gets more dogs
And the sheep crying out to each other
Until people buy more lamb chops
If I yell at night there's a reply of silence.

Revolutionary social work is loving and it is anti-oppressive. The basis for all anti-oppressive practice requires that interpersonal violence is addressed. Healing from interpersonal violence requires love. Healing also requires the violence to stop. I am not separate from the violence of my childhood and all the harm and injustice I have witnessed in my social work career. Love ethic informed values collectively can provide guidance for the ways forward in this urgent and complex moral task. This is the central obligation of the revolutionary social worker who is guided in their practice with values and ideas that are congruent with the love ethic model. The values need to be held in mind and heart during practice situations. The more complex, conflictual and dangerous (unsafe) the practice situation, the more crucial it is for the practitioner to use these values. The task is to scrutinise every action or non-action to ensure it has loving intentions and effects. Ethics is about the enacting of values in specific relationships and situations. The purpose is to address violence in all its forms of lovelessness and injustice.

Problematics of violence

This section defines violence and outlines some examples of interpersonal violence that can cause trauma, loss, oppression and death for individuals and groups.

Violence is the use, or threat of use, of force to control or hurt another person or animal or to degrade nature. For people, it can involve abuse in the form of emotional, physical, mental, financial, sexual, social, cultural and spiritual harm, harm to animals and pets, damage to property and technological (digital) abuse (DV Connect, 2019). It can also include harm to wild animals, farm animals, landscapes and ecosystems. Violence is a social issue because of the prevalence of harm caused by individuals who gain from patriarchal (male-dominated) and capitalist social structures, discriminatory attitudes and norms which condone violence (Dobash & Dobash, 1979; hooks, 2000a).

Responsibility for stopping interpersonal violence rests with the individuals who enact the violence, including dominant social groups (particularly white privileged heterosexual men), businesses and social institutions such as schools, the media, human service organisations and governments. For example, globally, violence of all kinds is recognised as the number one health issue for women which in turn highlights its gendered nature (World Health Organisation, WHO, 2013; Fitz-Gibbon & Maher, 2018). In this regard, there are differential and heightened patterns of victimisation for women with one or more of the following characteristics: Aboriginal or Torres Strait Islander, living in a rural or remote area, HIV positive, mental illness, incarcerated, lower socio-economic status and linguistically diverse (ANROWS, 2015).

Domestic violence

The terms of domestic (DV), family violence (FV) and intimate partner violence (IPV) are forms of interpersonal violence which usually involve men being violent towards women and children (Bryce, 2015, p. 7). According to Bryant & Bricknell (2017), in Australia one woman is murdered every week by her current or ex-partner. Violence by women against men and other women, and between men is also illegal, harmful and unethical behaviour.

The term "concurrent re-victimisation" refers to the link between domestic violence and sexual assault where research indicates that "women who experience child sexual abuse (CSA) are more likely to experience interpersonal sexual violence than women who have not experienced CSA. Similarly, women who have experienced CSA are more likely to experience DV (not limited to sexual violence) in their adult relationships" (Australia's National Research Organisation for Women's Safety, ANROWS, 2015, p. 2).

Research into womens' lived experience of DV during pregnancy, a recognised risk factor, is described by Baird in relation to Lisa who:

> Experienced physical violence prior to her pregnancy as well as other types of abusive behaviour, including emotional and controlling behaviour supported by extreme verbal violence. She stated that there was an escalation in the physical violence during her pregnancy, becoming more frequent and more brutal: 'It got worse after I was pregnant: he became much more physical, and it was as if being pregnant didn't make any difference to him'. Lisa

in fact endured many physical assaults during her pregnancy, with several visits to hospital as a result of her injuries, yet at no time was she ever asked whether her injuries were a result of domestic violence. (2015, pp. 30-31)

Child sexual assault

Australia's Attorney-General's Department defines child sexual assault as "any act which exposes a child to, or involves a child in, sexual processes beyond his or her understanding or contrary to accepted community standards [...]. It includes child grooming, which refers to actions deliberately undertaken with the aim of befriending and establishing an emotional connection with a child, to lower the child's inhibitions in preparation for sexual activity with the child" (2017a, p. 27). The 2017 report *Australian Royal Commission into Institutionalised Responses to Childhood Sexual Assault* contains survivors' accounts of their experiences. A total of 3,955 narratives were received and are presented in *Volume 5, Private Sessions of the Final Report*. For example:

From a young age, Romana was sexually and physically abused by her father, to the degree she experienced 'grievous bodily harm'. When she was around seven years old, in the mid-1960s, Romana's father committed suicide, so her mother moved the children to Sydney where she started attending the local Catholic school run by nuns. Attached to the school was a church from which two priests, Father Mullally and Father Calibri, ministered. Romana had not been attending the school for very long when one of the nuns requested she go to the presbytery. 'If a nun told you what to do you just did it [...] I just remember going in and there were two priests [...] I had my back to them washing up and one of them came behind me and sexually molested me [...] I think he was masturbating but I couldn't see, so I couldn't say for sure [...] I have no idea who it was.'

After that incident, Romana lost all interest in going to church. Because her mother had never intervened when she was being abused by her father, she did not disclose the priest's abuse. 'My mother chose not to see.' And because the abuse Romana experienced at the hands of her father was so traumatising, she has always regarded the priest's assault, although terrible, as much less impactful. (Attorney-General's Department, 2017b, n.p.)

Professional privilege used to control

Professional privilege refers to the advantages that accrue to a practitioner due to their professional status, income, legal authority and ability to influence others. Professional privilege is meant to be used to uphold the interests and wellbeing of service users. However, it can involve interpersonal violence. For example, service users and advocacy groups hold a critique towards mental health professions for the use of force and coercion in the treatment of people with a lived experience of mental illness (National Mental Health Consumers and Carers Forum, 2009; Tingleff, Bradley, Gilbert, Munksgaard & Houndsgaard, 2017). This can be the case for people who are subject to state legislation (Chavulak & Petrakis, 2017) and are therefore being detained against their wishes (Tochkov & Williams, 2018). Research shows that the use of seclusion and restraint increases the likelihood of violence and causes trauma to the person who is restrained or secluded (Lim, Wynaden & Heslop, 2018).

Burbank explains that violence in how he was treated was the most impactful issue in his efforts to recover from mental illness:

> I have known the inside of prisons with bars. I have also known the outside where it is still a prison with no bars. The hospitals where I have been an inpatient have usually had locked doors. The mental hospitals felt like prisons. However, the doors being locked did not help me feel safe. Both the custodial and therapeutic places were sites of many tyrannies for me – tyrannies in the name of control and care respectively. I felt more care when in prison – from other in-mates although often interlinked with violence. The violence in the locked hospitals was not named but madder in its effects on me because it had no name. (2014, p. 11)

Animal violence

Interpersonal violence also refers to violence enacted against animals by people. Animals who have an economic value to people experience violence, usually death. Sentient Media (2019) report that 200 million land animals are consumed each day globally with this number growing to 3 billion when wild and water animals are included. Additionally, some animals without economic value are also killed. For example, in the dairy industry, male calves are routinely killed at birth because it can "cost a farmer up to £30 per calf to sell it on for beef or veal, while early disposal costs just £9" (Levitt, 2018, n.p.).

These practices and language such as "early disposal" are indicative of a human-centric bias (Boetto, 2019) which objectifies animals. The objectification is institutionalised on a mass scale and makes possible the unfair treatment of whole species of animals (Eaglehawk, 2020).

Anonymous for the Voiceless is an animal activist group who promote an abolitionist approach. This approach argues that veganism is the required moral baseline (Francione, 2016; Francione & Charlton, 2013). Veganism involves nonviolence to animals, and refusing to use animals in any way that causes them discomfort, unsafety or unwillingness. Anonymous for the Voiceless (2019) undertake street activism such as 'Cube of truth' which graphically depicts farm animal suffering in videos on laptop screens held by masked protestors. Animals communicate with their whole bodies and the images show evident awareness of distress and suffering by the animals.

Ecological violence

Ecological or environmental violence occurs when an individual part of, or the entire, ecosystem is degraded beyond the ability of nature to recover and sustain life (White, 2017). In turn, environmental justice refers to an ecosystem's experience of equality, wellbeing, nonviolence, love and sustainability in all aspects of their life and situation. Some types of government or business infrastructure projects (Brady, 2020; Jecks, 2020) and industry such as large-scale animal farming and extractive (mining) operations (Cleary, 2017) have substantial degrading and unsustainable impacts on the environment. White (2009) explains that it constitutes a form of state crime if governments fail to act to protect the natural environment. The impacted ecosystems and life that depend on it can be understood as environmental victims who should be able to make claims for redress and compensation (White, 2009).

Cleary advocates on behalf of the environment when he gives an example of the dark side of Australia's resource boom:

> When seen for the first time from the air it looks as though a giant spiderweb has spread over what was until recently a vast patchwork of paddocks and fields. Like nothing ever before visited upon the continent of Australia, a network of wells, access roads, pipelines and pressurisation stations is fanning out across the Darling Downs. This is what coal-seam gas (CSG) looks like from above, beneath the surface it is even more intrusive [...] [it]

21

is the result of the 5,000 CSG wells installed so far, but this is just one-fifth to one-tenth of the likely number to be drilled into agricultural land in [...] [Queensland] by mid-century [...]. Three mammoth projects worth $70 billion are being built over 20,000 square kilometres of good cultivation and grazing land [...]. Based on overseas experience [...] the industry has the potential to [...] contaminate underground aquifers, produce billions of litres of unmanageable saline wastewater that will yield millions of tonnes of salt and threaten farmland, river systems and wetlands; [...] accelerate climate change; [...] trigger earthquakes; and, depress land values. (2017, pp. 20-23)

Doing no harm, professional integrity and acting with love

The baseline ethical position for the revolutionary social worker is nonviolence. In the helping professions this is usually referred to as "nonmaleficience" which means to not "wilfully harm [...] [individuals] and to refrain from actions that risk harm" (Canadian Counselling and Psychotherapy Association, 2007, p. 2). Beauchamp and Childress (1985/2013) explain that this means not acting in ways that would unnecessarily or unjustifiably cause harm. Matters of unequal power, context and understandings of harm all have a bearing on the upholding this value. Nonviolence theory explains that people have a moral obligation to nonviolently resist harm and violence (King, 1999). King, who worked alongside Martin Luther King Jr. during the American civil rights movement, writes:

> It is [...] [the] ability of nonviolent resistance to cause or intensify internal problems for the opponent that places nonviolent action in a special category among the techniques of struggle. Disagreement by the populace with the brutal measures witnessed 'turns on itself', and the conflict shifts. It becomes, instead, an internal dispute with the regime or adversary over its infliction of violence on unarmed peaceful protesters. (1999, p. xvi)

The intensifying of internal problems for the actioner of violence is a moral pressure and should not be conflated with the nonviolent protesters causing harm to the high power actors. Rather, hooks (2000a) places the willingness to enable one's own or another's moral good at the centre of love ethic work. It is not a moral good to oppress people or repress their collective calls for justice.

Most social workers will at some point be in contexts where they are confronted with violence or have to protect themselves and others by using force. For this reason love ethic work needs to show how to respond to issues of coercion and issues of potential direct violence, respectively. The line of argument here is an example of the need for public education in nonviolence and love. The book provides a starting point to this educational goal through an emphasis on applying the love ethic to build nonviolent, loving, just and trauma informed relationships. These relationships may be with individuals and groups in households, workplaces, organisations, communities and animals' home places.

The book also emphasises the importance of social workers taking responsibility for the ethical and substantive quality of their practice. This is integral to professional integrity which is recognised as a key social work value (Australian Association of Social Workers, AASW, 2010, p. 13). Banks and Gallagher (2009) suggest it is the value upon which all others rely. Professional integrity is closely related to "ethical use of self" (Kaushik, 2017, p. 21) where practitioners consciously cultivate their capabilities and qualities of being a good person as the main resource for their professional work. Professional integrity is not a once and for all achieved state and, therefore, needs to be cultivated 'in situ' where the complexities of context, relationships and power are able to be considered. In a similar way Banks describes this as "identity work" which involves working on one's professional identity to be an "ethically good person" (2016, p. 37). Identity work also needs to include self-development practices as citizens where there is no disjuncture between the private self and professional self. Self-development work is not a straightforward intellectual exercise as it involves "emotion work". Banks describes this as managing one's emotions and ensuring that engagement with others is premised on caring emotions (2016, p. 37). It is not a matter of managing emotions in a controlling way, rather it is a matter of cultivating emotional intelligence as an ongoing commitment (Bloom & Farragher, 2013). This is about the "emotional labour" of professional practice where:

> An emotionally intelligent worker manages a difficult situation by [...] keeping your voice down and containing your own threat responses, and not emotionally escalating on the inside, even when a child or adult is cursing you, spitting at you, or threatening you with bodily harm [...] which requires a level of self-control and emotional management that is well [...] amazing. (Bloom & Farragher, 2013, p. 169)

To refuse to hate or retaliate and to seek a compassionate understanding of the situation paves the way for the practitioner to act with love. Love is not a word typically used to describe the purpose of social work (Hughes, 2018) and a discourse on love is largely absent in social work publications (Godden, 2016). However, love as action with a low power individual or group in their interests is implicit in all social work codes of ethics. It is explicit in just one – the Swedish social work *Code of Ethics* which links the principle of human dignity to love by describing this principle as a declaration of love for people (Swedish Union for Social Sciences Professionals, 2015, pp. 5-6). Love informed practice means there is an ongoing conscious commitment to cultivating professional integrity that is founded on doing no harm and acting with love in all situations. When this commitment is maintained by all actors in situations of violence, there will be an increase in experiences of safety, wellbeing and justice.

Values for love ethic informed relationships

For relationship-focused practice where the individual or group is impacted by violence further ethical guidance is provided by an interrelated set of love ethic informed values. The terms individual and group are inclusive of humans, animals and specific ecosystems or the totality of nature. The term love ethic informed identifies a congruence between the specific value, idea or practice and the love ethic model. The Glossary provides definitions of these and other key ideas in the book.

Bodily autonomy

The idea of violence includes human-against-human violence, human-against-animal violence and human-against-nature violence. The minimal indicator of violence is intrusion against an individual's or group's bodily autonomy and the experiencing of harm as a result. Intrusions against bodily autonomy will interrelate with emotional, mental and social experiences of harm (Bloom, 2017) for the individual or group. Therefore, bodily autonomy is a characteristic of a sovereign being who has an intrinsic right to be respected and treated with love and nonviolence. Bodily autonomy also refers to nonhuman animals, land and seascapes and all aspects of the materiality of nature.

Safe relationships

According to Bloom (2017) a safe relationship is where the individuals in an interaction are experiencing physical, psychological and moral safety. When these forms of safety are present social safety is able to be fostered and maintained. The dynamics of power, context, time and specificities surrounding an interaction can intricately impact perceptions of safety in relationships. For example, a perceived safe interaction can at a later point in time be reviewed and interpreted as unsafe when new information comes to light. In unequal and abusive situations, the low power individual or group is more likely to experience unsafety. They are also less likely to be heard if they show concern about being treated unfairly and being hurt or feeling unsafe.

Safe spaces

Safety in relationships requires safe places for people to meet and engage in "courageous conversations" (D'Aunno & Heinz, 2017, p. 3) about matters of concern. A safe space is both about the physical location or context where space is synonymous with place and amenity, and more importantly about the conditions of the interactive environment between unequal individuals. Bhabha writes about the "third space" (1994, p. 2) which can be understood as a meeting place where there is no exploitation or violence. In this space low power groups seek justice through dialogue with high power groups. Safe spaces also refers to the need to protect environments and habitats for animals and for the sustainability of life (Poelina, 2020).

Self-love, love of other people, love of animals and nature

hooks (2001) explains that where there is love there will be no oppression. Elsewhere she argues that if policy-makers placed the love ethic at the centre of their decision-making there would be no lovelessness and inequality (hooks, 2000b). Godden draws on hooks' love ethic and identifies the range of ways love can be expressed as love of self and family, love for colleagues, love for communities, including service users, love of nature and spiritual love (2017, pp. 413-414). Leading with love in relationships involves compassion linked to a critical understanding of power issues and relevant individuals being enabled to take responsibility for their actions.

Lived experience and narrative

A key love ethic value is the honouring of the individual's lived experience as valid knowledge and as that individual's truth (for example, Our Consumer Place, 2011, p. 9). This positionality in turn places emphasis on listening to and being influenced by the individual's narrative or story. Isay, founder and president of the StoryCorp Project, claims that "listening is an act of love" (2016, n.p.). StoryCorp is an oral history initiative in America that has gathered tens of thousands of everyday peoples' stories and validated them by storing the stories in the Library of Congress and sharing excerpts on public radio. The Dulwich Centre in Adelaide, Australia, has developed a rich narrative practice approach which believes justice and healing occurs through listening to peoples' stories (Morgan, 2000).

Emotionality, nonverbal knowing and materiality

The love ethic approach values emotionality (Furtak, 2018) as well as rationality and nonverbal (Berry & Pennebaker, 1993; Meyer & Forkman, 2015) as well as verbal experience and ways of knowing. These capacities reflect the richness and diversity between people and between people and nonhuman beings. This positionality seeks to avoid the bias in dualistic thinking where the non dominant expressions (e.g. emotionality) tend to be linked to non dominant social groups (e.g. women) and species groups (Plumwood, 2000). The bias can be used to justify control and mistreatment by dominant groups.

Violence and trauma have material effects on the individual in terms of bodily impacts and flows on to have intricate influences in the individual's life situation. This includes effects on the individual's mental health, financial security, employment, housing, relationships and social status (Clarke, Barnes and Ross, 2018). For farm animals, violence has material effects on their bodies, lack of freedom of movement and ability to survive. For wild animals the bodily and material impacts of violence tend to occur through natural disasters and the destruction of habitat and ecosystems which has flow on effects of loss and threat to animals (Reality Check Team, BBC News, 2020). Braidotti calls for a different kind of subjectivity which is "relational, embodied and embedded, affective and accountable" (2018, p. 1). This would hold a tension with the mind-body split which devalues embodiment in favour of rationality. Braidotti's (2018) posthuman subjectivity also addresses the nature-culture split which devalues the material nature of beingness and the interconnectedness of species, plants and other matter. Haraway (2015) suggests the term of "natureculture" to avoid this dualism.

Active participation and voice

Active participation is a form of social responsibility where low power individuals and groups are empowered and proactive in contributing to matters of importance to them. Freire (1970) explains that the oppressed have an obligation to name the world and to empower themselves to break the culture of silence that occurs in situations of oppression. He describes this as a political activity of coming to voice, of speaking and being heard, through conscientisation processes of critical reflecting and acting in order to change the world (Freire, 1970). This can be an onerous responsibility for low power individuals and groups as they will already be experiencing the impacts of disadvantage. There is no guarantee they will be able to influence high power interest groups to engage in non exploitative dialogue. Nevertheless, seeking to influence power and governance structures is crucial in unequal contexts. This is because the powerful groups will not readily give up their privileges and socio-political advantages (Mullaly & West, 2017; Thompson, 2018).

Responsibility

Responsibility refers to the ability to respond in a relevant way in a given situation and with the actors' respective interests, influence and privilege being critically analysed to understand the order of responsibility that accrues to each actor. Accountability is closely related to the type of responsibility that is required by high power individuals and groups to address harm that they have caused or have failed to act to prevent (Ross, 2020). This is a high order responsibility in a moral sense because of the harm that is impacting low power individuals and groups. The harm can include adverse impacts on people, animals and ecosystems and can threaten quality of life, survival and sustainability.

Other important love ethic informed values

A number of other important values such as transformational change leadership, ecojustice, sustainability, stewardship, dialogue, trauma informed practice and inclusive governance are discussed in the next chapter as some of the main components of the love ethic model.

Conclusion

The book commenced by posing the idea of revolutionary love as the purpose of social work. It was followed by conveying how the personal and professional is political for the author with the use of a sociological poetic. Some examples of the problematics of violence were outlined to locate loving revolutionary practice in relationships and situations of violence and harm. The chapter identified a set of values that are congruent with causing no harm, maintaining professional integrity and acting with love. The identified values are integral to building a capacity for love-based practice to address violence at the interpersonal level of interactions with people, animals and nature. The values provide guidance for the revolutionary social worker where some may be more relevant or pressing to act upon depending on the situation.

Chapter 2
The love ethic model in social work

The book is unique in the social work literature as it presents a guide for how to practice ethically in complex, violent, loveless and unjust situations by outlining the love ethic model. The model for practice takes as its starting point that social workers can contribute to fostering love in their personal and professional lives. Each and every act of love, which enfolds nonviolence and justice, matters and combines to form the person's ethical integrity. The love ethic model shows how to do justice work to lovingly resist, challenge and change violence, hate or lovelessness and injustice into nonviolence, love and fairness.

The first articulation of the love ethic model was presented in the edited publication by Ross, Brueckner, Palmer and Eaglehawk (2020) and derives from the influential work of hooks (1994, 2000a, 2000b, 2001, 2008). hooks (2000a) explains that where there is love there will be no oppression. This offers a challenge to social work to centre a love ethic in its commitment to social justice. The book provides a guide to applying ethics with a model that integrates and re-interprets social work ethics and skills for revolutionary practice.

The love ethic model is influenced by: feminism including eco-feminism; the critical and anti-oppressive social work literature; anti-racist, postcolonialist and Indigenous ideas; animal rights and posthumanism; and, ecology and environmentalism. Writers in these traditions are utilised throughout the book. The love ethic model provides ethical interpretations of the main goals implied by these theories, namely the goals of nonviolence, love and ecojustice. Thus, it is not a theory book or an analysis of social issues book. Rather, the book is about how to understand and apply anti-oppressive ideas using the key goals of the influential anti-oppressive theories and translating them into ethical guidelines for practice. Violence can be changed to nonviolence by using nonviolence. Lovelessness can be changed to love by using love. Injustice can be changed to justice by using justice. In these ways, anti-oppressive ideas informed by the love ethic when enacted comprise the potential for revolutionary practice.

Thus, the book provides a model of already integrated, ready-to-use values, theories and skills for revolutionary practice. Revolutionary practice is a broad field of approaches that have in common the anti-oppressive skills of challenging, resisting and changing oppressive situations with love, nonviolence and justice. These three main skills involve any actions, or decisions to not act, which uphold the love ethic where resistance is the minimum responsibility required in the face of oppression. Resistance may not declare itself and could look like acquiescence, but it is in fact a "creative transgression of limits" (Chokr, 2004, p. 3) in unsafe situations. Chokr (2004) explains that resistance is therefore any nonviolent act that seeks to protect the actor or others and to defend them from intrusions against their autonomy and rights.

The book supports a "politicisation of ethics" (Valdiva, 2002, p. 430) to unsettle master narratives because as Lorde (1979/2018) famously declared "the master's tools will never dismantle the master's house." hooks explains that feminist theory needs to be relevant to people and their pain and anguish caused by "the profound and unrelenting misery and sorrow" of male domination (1994, p. 75). The book supports hooks' belief that theory can be a healing place (1994, p. 59) by suggesting that the love ethic model shows how this can be done.

Ethical practice is about being a good person who consciously cultivates virtues of character such as courage and honesty. Aristotle explains "that in any situation, there is always the right thing to do. To determine which, one needs practical intelligence that is nothing else but an intellectual quality of a good human" (cited in Bykova, 2016, p. 448). In terms of the book, it is about how you, the reader, understand and negotiate your "individualised biography" (Howard, 2007, p. 25), your identity and the positionality (Ortega, 2017) you take in a particular practice situation. For present purposes, positionality is used to refer to the combined influence of each person's beliefs, biography, relationship with others, lived experiences, and the specificities of time, embodiment, place and context. Fook describes this as the person's "reflexive stance" (2016, p. 56) which is tied to reflective thinking and the ability to be self-aware 'in situ' and to be able, thereby, to notice the influences of their own positionality in practice. Fook (2016) has written extensively about critical reflection as thinking and analysis skills where the practitioner seeks an understanding of power dynamics and context influences to address oppression. Fook argues that "a critical reflective approach holds the potential for emancipatory practices [...] in that it first questions and disrupts dominant structures and relations and lays the ground for change" (2016, p. 54). Revolutionary practice builds on this "ground for change" to realise the emancipatory potential of expressions of loving ethics in situations of violence, lovelessness and injustice.

Finally, it is important to acknowledge that identity and thereby positionality, are socially constructed and socially mediated experiences (Berger & Luckmann, 1967). The identity of a person may be individualised as unique to the person and at the same time it is more than an internal psychological phenomenon separate to society. The idea of "intersubjectivity" brings attention to the socially created nature of being and as such the transpersonal nature of experiences, including identity (Stevanovic & Koski, 2018). Further, individuals – people, animals and ecosystems - are embodied, they have bodies, and experience the world in material or physical, as well as emotional, spiritual and ecological dimensions (Braidotti, 2018). The relational nature of being creates the individual's positionality for engaging with others in specific historical and geographical contexts.

This means ethics is a social practice between individuals who to some extent co-create the micro dynamics of the context in which they interact. I will guide you in 'trying on' a love ethic approach and invite you to critically reflect on it in terms of goodness-of-fit with your positionality in some exemplar scenarios (see Chapter 3).

Influences in creation of the love ethic model

This section outlines some of the influences and ideas that bring me to writing the book at this time, as a new decade begins. The pathway to an articulation of the love ethic model has been an individual one of my personal journey and life work. It has also been a collective one with other people, as paths have intersected in a myriad of ways over many decades. Some of my biggest teachers have been people in client and student roles, trees, animals and "Earth Mother" (Duncan-Kemp cited in Sutton, 2010) in all her dynamic beingness. For the moment, though, the focus is on people who have influenced my development of the love ethic model through their writing, research and activism. The chapter also introduces key ideas and foci which have formed the love ethic model in its current iteration.

The love ethic model is a relationship-based approach to working with others to challenge, resist and change violence, lovelessness and injustice. How did I get to this succinct statement? If I were asked – 'what is the main organising idea?' - I would answer that it is about life (and death) being experienced in relationships. The centering of relationships as the space where hurt and therefore healing can happen is seemingly a self-evident truth. However, I experienced a shift in its meaning early in my social work career with Buber's (1970) idea of the I-You relationship. According to Buber "the basic word I-You establishes the world of relation" (1970, p. 56). It implies that reality is in the between – for example, between me as the writer and you as the reader. He explains that there are three areas in which the "world of relation arises", namely, with nature, with humans and in life with spiritual beings (Buber, 1970, pp. 56-57). Buber's ideas are similar to many Indigenous worldviews that are premised on an ecological schema which locates humans in the natural world, not separate from it (Poelina, 2020).

Buber (1970) explains that within the three areas of experience, there are two types of relation, namely, "I-It" and "I-You" relationships. The I-You relationship is where individuals are treated with equal intrinsic value and respect. Buber writes that "relation is reciprocity" (1970, p. 67). There is no exploitation or use of the individual and dialogue for mutual benefit becomes possible. The I-It relationship is indicative of oppressive uses of power by the 'I' against a being who is dehumanised and becomes the 'It', the "other" (Seidman, 2016, p. 309), the lesser valued individual. It is only in going back to re-read Buber for the book, that I gained a new appreciation of how he places love in the centre of his philosophy. Buber writes that "love is a cosmic force" where "love is a responsibility of an I for a You" (1970, p. 66). He explains that love is not any specific feeling, it is about the equality that occurs in love relationships "from the smallest to the greatest" (Buber, 1970, p. 66). Love tends to be juxtaposed with hatred but Buber elaborates that a person who hates directly is "closer to a relation than those who are without love and hate" (1970, p. 68). The book shows how to appeal to dominating individuals' and groups' higher sense of morality, their good, to invite them into relationship to take responsibility for any harm they have caused or condoned. Thus, in

Buberian terms, the book gives guidance in how to apply the love ethic model to enable revolutionary social work with others to change from I-It relationships to I-You reciprocal and loving relationships.

I-You relationships form the basis for genuine dialogue between equals to address ethical concerns of harm, loss and unsustainability. Freire links dialogue and love when he explains that "love is at the same time the foundation of dialogue and dialogue itself [...] if I do not love life [...] if I do not love people – I cannot enter into dialogue" (1970, pp. 70-71). The love ethic model enables the practitioner to undertake dialogical praxis with other parties to co-create loving responses to oppressive situations. Dialogical praxis involves loving and critical reflection-action cycles as the basis of justice work (Freire, 1970, p. 68). This requires I-You relationships between the parties who collaborate without exploitation in group-based processes.

Finally, Leonard calls on social workers to contribute to the "reconstructing of the emancipatory project" of welfare (1997, p. 30) which is consistent with the goals of the revolutionary social worker. He warns of the traps that can occur for the "modern expert [of the state]" who adopts an "ethic of responsibility to act" believing they are acting in the interests of people in service user roles (hereafter service users). Leonard continues that "in the place of the will to control and homogenise, postmodern ethics asserts a responsibility to Otherness [...] by clearing a space for the voices of those [people and animals] [...] who have been reduced to objects, have never spoke as active subjects, but who have always been acted upon by those [professionals] [...] with knowledge" (1997, p. 151). The book shows how to practice in non controlling, non surveilling and non assimilating ways so that the revolutionary social worker is not a new name for old tyrannies and failures of professional responsibility.

Love, justice and social work

There is only limited literature on the place of love in social work despite its significance in activism for transformational social change (Godden, 2018). Butot (2004) suggests that love has tended to be understood as compassion and empathy with these capacities in turn being treated as technical skills. Hughes (2018) claims that love is a neglected concept but one that could contribute to holding an ethical tension with the limits of care in human service organisations. Nussbaum (2013) argues that love is necessary for justice work to ensure a deep connection with oppressed individuals' and groups' dignity and humanity. Without this deep loving connection and engagement, it is easier to justify tyrannical actions and violence (Nussbaum, 2013) or to blame the harmed people for the unjust situations (Baum, 2018).

Anti-oppressive theories explain how dominating groups use their privilege and power at the expense of dominated groups (hooks, 2000b; Freire, 1970; Fook, 2016). Fook writes that "domination is structural yet it also is experienced personally" and therefore requires an awareness of power relations and an ability to challenge ruling groups (2016, p. 18). The purpose of justice struggles is to achieve accountability for violence and harm done by dominating individuals and groups. Freire (1970) warns that the enactors of violence will resist invitations to dialogue with the oppressed and will avoid being accountable for injustice. A deep moral question which arises is, how to respond to violence without resorting to violence? An international review of struggles for justice shows that large scale mobilisation of oppressed people is more likely to occur and to be effective if it is nonviolent (Chenoweth & Stephan, 2011). The will to be nonviolent comes from the will to love and a refusal to hate (Abuelaish, 2012).

A love ethic encompasses a range of nonviolent ideas and socio-political capacities that includes caring for and caring about people with a critical understanding of the politics of care (Pease, Vreugdenhil & Stanford, 2018). The social work literature shows an appreciation of an ethic of care (Banks, 2012, 2016) which values relationship, kindness and the enabling of responsibility in relationships. The idea of care is also a personal quality in virtue-based ethics (Banks & Gallagher, 2009; Gray, 2009) which suggests an individual can cultivate personal attributes that enable ethical practice. Pease, Vreugdenhil and Stanford (2018) introduce the notion of a critical ethic of care to describe a range of anti-oppressive practice responses to social harm and injustice. Additionally, they explain that a critical ethic of care values relationships that are mutual and trustworthy as a counter to the individualism of neoliberalism (Pease, Vreugdenhil and Stanford, 2018).

In outlining how love has been a topic of interest in international social work, Hughes (2018) acknowledges Canadian researcher, Butot (2004), who explores social workers' understanding of love from a critical perspective. Butot's research developed the idea of "love as emancipatory praxis" which values intersubjectivity and justice work that is inclusive of planet Earth (Butot, 2004, p. 101). Thus, the full implication of the love ethic extends caring to animals (Ryan, 2011) and the planet (Mies & Shiva, 1993; Shiva, 2014; Plumwood, 1993, 2000, 2002).

An explicit consideration of love is gaining some recognition in Australia's professional journal for social workers – *Australian Social Work*. Godden (2017) presents hooks' love ethic as a radical theory for social work practice. Godden draws on the ideas of hooks to claim that the love ethic is a "model of relationship-based activism" (2017, p. 405). Godden (2017) argues that the promise of an ethic of love in social work is its emancipatory potential which can be enacted through: self-love and family love; love of colleagues; love for community; love for humanity, including service users; love for nature; and, spiritual love. Godden (2016, 2018) applied her ideas about love by using collaborative inquiry research and community engagement strategies to support workers and residents in a rural community in Timor-Leste to explore what love means to them.

My writing provides another Australian example of the love ethic in social work in the form of research and community support strategies over almost twenty years in the small town of Yarloop in Western Australia. The research was conducted in the period 2002 - 2004 to enable dialogue and problem-solving related to a range of health, social and environmental impacts on local communities by the Alcoa alumina refinery near Yarloop (Ross, 2013; Brueckner & Ross, 2010). An initial formulation of a love ethic model was developed from the research that can be used by social activists to respond to failures of corporate social responsibility by holding high power individuals accountable (Ross, 2017). This earlier formulation of the love ethic model was further refined drawing on the insights of eco-activists (Ross et al., 2020) with a predominant focus of ecological conflict.

Love and nonviolence as integral to international justice struggles

Hughes (2018) acknowledges that love is understood by some of the greatest leaders for social change as a powerful and potentially transformational resource. It can unite people for nonviolent struggles across boundaries of class, race, culture and country. The revolutionary leaders who have been influential in my practice are introduced and acknowledged here. Mahatma Gandhi was a lawyer who based his leadership style on self-discipline and living his talk of nonviolence and compassion (Bakshi, 2013). Gandhi used the Hindu and Buddhist term "ahimsa" for love and linked it with "satyagraha" which means nonviolence and he believed "there could be no ahimsa if compassion, forgiveness and equality were absent" (Gandhi, 2013, pp. 114-115). His leadership approach was premised on nonviolent acts of civil disobedience and non co-operation against the British government in the decades of struggle for India's freedom from colonialist rule (Gandhi, 2013). Nonviolence refers to the peaceful, respectful and tactical use of power and influence to pressure high power individuals and groups to uphold the protesters' justice claims. It can include a broad range of nonviolent direct action strategies such as street marches, media campaigns, petitions, sit-ins, strikes and non co-operation (Sharp, 2005). Nonviolence works best when citizens are given training in nonviolence if they are intending to participate in public rallies and high-risk activities (see examples in Brady, 2020).

Many leaders in struggles for justice and freedom followed in Gandhi's footsteps and adopted nonviolence and love as their ethical compass. Martin Luther King Junior was a Baptist minister in the city of Montgomery, Alabama during the racial segregation era in America's southern states. King preached the Christian message of "love your enemies, bless them that curse you, do good to them that hate you" (Saint Matthew, cited in King, 1957, p. 316). He believed that "love will save our world, love even for enemies" (King, 1957, p. 316).

South African freedom leader and later President of South Africa, Nelson Mandela, writes in his influential autobiography "I wanted South Africa to see that I loved even my enemies" and "no-one is born hating another person because of the colour of [...] their skin, or [...] their [...] religion. People must learn to hate, and if they learn to hate, they can be taught to love" (2013, p. 568; pp. 621-622).

bell hooks is an English professor and black feminist activist whose writing exposes the injustice of dominant white culture and white supremacy discourses. She grew up in America during the civil rights movement and was influenced by King's use of nonviolence and civil disobedience to challenge racism. She writes about a culture of lovelessness in black communities in America and claims lovelessness is occurring because of a societal failure to place a love ethic at the centre of socio-economic policy considerations and implementation (hooks, 2000a). hooks (1994) explains that the ethic of love brings people to an increased concern for issues of domination and injustice. It also brings people to a desire to understand and challenge the interconnected nature of systems of domination (hooks, 1994). Additionally, she recognises the intersectionality between the lack of environmental sustainability, class and racial inequality (hooks, 2008). Elsewhere, hooks defines an ethic of love as "one that is exemplified by the combined forces of care, respect, knowledge and responsibility" (2001, pp. 4-5). hooks (2001) explains that love is about extending ourselves or others for their highest good. It is about the learning needed by dominating groups to understand the impact, for example, of racism and to undertake decolonising work.

In Australia, I want to acknowledge the important Indigenous activism and writing by Anne Poelina (2020), Michael Woodley (2020) and in the social work academic space, Bindi Bennett and Sue Green (2019). Bennett and Green's writing focuses on sharing First Nation People's language and knowledge to promote cultural responsiveness and the decolonising of Australian society and social work. Green (2018) explains that according to the Wiradyuri People care is central to the belief that people and the environment are not separate. "Yindyamarra" refers to the moral obligation to show "respect and honour [and to] go slowly, go gently" and "Wirimbirragu Ngurambanggu" means "caring for country" (Green, 2018, p. 141). Green (2018) writes that under "buyaa" (lore) it is an offence not to provide for others. It is about a way of life and Green calls on all Australians to understand and work within these values. Bennett and her colleagues claim that social work with First Nation People has tended to be "intrusive, judgemental, controlling and harmful", creating intergenerational trauma due to social work's part, for example, in the Stolen Generations (Green, Bennett, Collins, Gowans, Hennessey & Smith, 2013, p. 207).

Bennett (2019) calls on social work as a profession to undertake decolonising work to understand and address the impact of its predominantly white privilege and to make possible truly collaborative and healing relationships with First Nation People. Poelina describes decolonisation as "a process that requires diversity in dialogue to build action and transformational change based on mutual respect and critical reflection" (2020, p. x). The love ethic model shows some ways for social workers to progress this pressing anti-oppressive work.

Redefining justice and including sustainability

The love ethic model recognises the intersectionality between people, animals and the environment (Gaard, 2011) and shows how to respond to the diversity of individuals and groups who may experience violence and injustice. Thus, social justice needs to be redefined to include the shift from social work's predominantly human-centric bias (Boetto, 2019) to an ecological paradigm. The International Federation of Social Work (2018) defines social justice as the respect for difference, equality, fair policies and freedom from oppression and discrimination, solidarity and social inclusion between social groups. Fraser (2009) defines justice as processes which include impacted and interested parties, or their representatives (for animals and the environment), as equal moral participants in understanding the justice concern and seeking its resolution. The term ecological justice or ecojustice incorporates social justice, species justice and environmental justice. Ecojustice refers to individuals and groups who have equal intrinsic value and whose rights and interests are protected and respected.

Ecojustice is inter-related with sustainability which involves three dimensions:

> The social dimension of society which shows as equality between people and between people and animals;

> The economic dimension of society which shows as nonviolence and non exploitation between business owners, governments and wealthy citizens and other people and animals; and,

> The environmental dimension of society which shows as mutual respect, love and justice between people and animals, all nonhuman beings and the natural world.

There are complex but direct relationships between all forms of justice and all types of sustainability. Sustainability issues need to be addressed for all types of justice to be realised. Social justice requires sustainability in social, economic and environmental domains. Significantly, social sustainability will provide the basis for other types of sustainability. It is the impact of humans as a species which has created an overburdening of nature's capacity to regenerate (Suzuki, 1997; Moore, 2016). Therefore, it is the social dimension that creates the pivot opportunities for a different relationship with nature. Power elites create inequality, gain disproportionately and, therefore, hold a higher order level of responsibility to address unsustainability. Species justice becomes possible if social justice is achieved, but should be sought in its own right, in parallel. A moral shift is required by people en mass to stop the consumption of some species of animals. All species of animals need to be equal and loved for species justice.

Environmental justice is crucial for all species' survival and justice. It becomes possible if social justice is achieved, but should be sought in its own right, in parallel. Environmental justice is not possible if a society's economy is reliant on the exploitation of the natural world.

In broad terms, unsustainability is occurring where the needs and rights of future generations (animals as well as people) and the ability of planet Earth to regenerate are compromised (Ross, 2015). This compromise occurs by the exploitation of minority groups (hereafter low power groups Hyde, 2018) including animals, and the degradation of nature (Suzuki, 1997; Moore, 2016) by the power elites of industry, government and other social structures (Mills, 1953). Unsustainability is a sign of ethical issues that link back to the three underlying oppressive relationship dynamics of violence, lovelessness and eco-injustice. While people are placed in the centre of actors with regard to issues of sustainability, it is not meant to convey that nature and animals are passive or inconsequential actors (Poelina, 2020). Rather, the argument is presented that all citizens and in particular, members of social groups who have extremes of privilege, power and wealth (hereafter high power groups Hyde, 2018), have a different order of responsibility to address ethical issues. Privilege refers to the unearned advantage of dominant groups (Pease, 2010) and is problematic when it is used to reinforce oppressive power relationships.

White (2009) claims it is a state crime if governments do not act to protect the environment from industries which prosper from exploiting natural resources and suggests there are nonhuman victims in such situations. For example, unsustainability is apparent in relation to the global reach of environmental issues and the loss of biodiversity (International Science-Policy Platform on Biodiversity and Ecosystem Services, 2019) and in conflicts between communities and the mining industry (Ross & Puccio, 2020; Woodley, 2020). Thus, social sustainability refers to equality in relationships between people (Ross, 2015) and between people and animals in families, groups, organisations, businesses, communities and environments. Social sustainability is present when there is love, nonviolence and justice in these relationships. Economic sustainability is created through social relationships and involves a social system of production and exchange of goods and services that respects and protects the environment. Further, economic sustainability disallows extreme wealth based on social disadvantage and exclusion (Australian Council of Social Services, ACOSS, 2018), species exploitation and environment degradation.

As such this responsibility brings with it the moral obligation to join with First Nation People in the stewardship of nature (Poelina, 2020). The idea of stewardship rests on the understanding that "country [...] [is] alive, vibrant and all encompassing [...] [and thus is] an active participant in the world and fully connected in a vast web of dynamic, interdependent relationships. These relationships are strong and resilient when they are maintained" (Poelina, 2020, p. ix). The fostering of sustainability is at the heart of the responsibility of stewardship.

Addressing anthropocentric harm with love

Every social, economic and environmental issue is an ethical issue and will involve complexities of violence, lovelessness and eco-injustice. The intersectionality of ethical issues can create harm, loss and suffering for low power groups of people, animals and ecosystems. In an argument for species justice, Eaglehawk suggests that the common thread in all types of oppression can be understood as "anthropocentric harm" (2020, p. 102). This is consistent with White's (2009) theory of green victimology that suggests any being who is oppressed is the victim of a crime. The idea of anthropocentric harm keeps the focus of the responsibility on humans as a species who have caused harm ranging from interpersonal and interspecies violence to ecological and global level adverse impacts. For example, Braidotti claims that the dominance of humans has become a "geological force with a planetary impact" (2013, p. 5). Deep ecologist, Macy (2019), describes the interconnectedness of all beings and life and describes the planetary harm of the current epoch as multidimensional, spanning material and spiritual realms.

The three main organising ideas and ethical goals in the love ethic model are nonviolence, love and ecojustice. In combination, they provide a different approach to articulating and responding to the seemingly intractable wicked problems confronting the world. Wicked problems are issues that arise from complex interactions between social, economic and environmental systems (Palmer, 2015, p. 578). For example, the wicked problem of violence against people with mental illness (Ross, 2014; Palmer & Ross, 2014), has no immediate, singular answer or specific responsible entity. The moral sophistication of a society can be measured by how well the most vulnerable people, animals and ecosystems are treated. In another example, the animal rights organisation, People for Ethical Treatment of Animals (PETA), quote Gandhi who "taught that nonviolence begins with what we eat. "To my mind", he said, "I hold that the more helpless a creature, the more entitled they are to protection by [...] [people] from the cruelty of [...] [people]" (2019, n.p.).

The highest expressions of public interest and morality involve the exercise of nonviolence, love and ecojustice by citizens in the specifics of their life and work circumstances. Therefore, the book supports ethical pluralism (McAuliffe, 2014) provided there is no harm, hatred or injustice occurring. That is to say, a wide path of ethical behaviour is consistent with the love ethic model which leaves room for conversions to love (hooks, 2000a). Conversions to love require high power actors to change through self-reflection in relation to how they use their power and privilege. The self-reflection needs to lead to learning and undertaking anti-oppressive actions to address the harm. However, persisting behaviours or patterns of harm cannot be condoned and need to be challenged, resisted and changed.

The book also takes its lead from Ryan's (2011) moral argument that social work needs to uphold the equal intrinsic value of all species, humans and nonhuman animals. It thereby supports his proposal for re-crafting social workers' codes of ethics to be inclusive of animals. Ryan writes that by defining social work's value of respect for people as one that includes all individuals and hence all species, social work can begin to address its human-centric bias (2011, p. 165). Francione and Charlton (2013) argue that the ethical stance of no harm to all species of animals requires the practice of veganism whereby animals are not used, abused or killed for research, human entertainment or consumption. This is just one example of the challenge for social workers where personal practices such as eating animals can conflict with professional values of non harm and species equality (Ross, Bennett & Menyweather, forthcoming).

Finally and significantly, the book extends this notion of equal intrinsic value to other individuals and natural entities as recognised by First Nation People (Poelina, 2020; Martin, 2003). There are precedents in law for natural entities such as rivers to be granted the same rights as people. In one example this involved 140 years of negotiations by the Te Awa Tupna traditional owners of the Whanganni River in New Zealand (Ainge Roy, 2017). In turn, the book does not concur with society elites' claims that their businesses should be granted personhood status and the same rights as humans (Khoury & Whyte, 2017). Nor does the book's ethical stance concur with the capitalist notion that the government should be preoccupied with ensuring a strong economy even if this comes at the expense of low power groups. The economy tends to be reified and prioritised and thereby provides the logic and legitimacy in capitalist societies for the wealthy elites of business to pursue their profit-driven interests without being accountable for the impact this has on the host society (White, 2018).

The love ethic model in social work

Eco-values and responsibilities

I recently substantially articulated the love ethic model by drawing on the insights from eco-activists' stories of justice work in the context of the strongly pro-development state of Western Australia (Ross, 2020). The common guiding values in all the eco-activists' justice work were identified as nonviolence, love and ecojustice (Ross, Brueckner, Palmer & Eaglehawk 2020). The eco-activists undertook a range of nonviolent direct action (NVDA) strategies, public campaigns and community art which variously sought to resist, challenge and change oppressive circumstances (see for example, Seiver, 2020). The common task for the eco-activists consisted of enabling low power groups to take responsibility to actively participate and raise their voices about the impacting justice issues. At the same time, high power individuals and groups who gained from the injustice or have caused it, were invited to take accountability and to include impacted parties in the governance processes. The responsibilities of stewardship of the environment and its sustainability were major concerns as the eco-activists were challenging how the natural environment and animals were being used and exploited (Brueckner & Ross, 2020). The overarching goal of justice work in the Ross et al. (2020) book was to uphold the public interest which refers to the best possible outcome for impacted parties and the sustainability of ecosystems.

Love ethic method as dialogical praxis

The love ethic practice method was developed from this justice work which had a predominantly community-based orientation and activism in relation to ecological conflict (Ross, 2020). It is presented here in an adapted form for the social work focus of the current book. The earlier articulation of the love ethic model focused on how to engage communities, governments and mining corporations. This justice work was typically undertaken using dialogical group work to engage the parties in addressing the injustices where ecological conflict was occurring. It is adapted here to bring a focus to addressing interpersonal violence between people-people, people-animals and people-the natural world. Dialogical praxis is undertaken by leadership focused on transformational change and involves any individual-with-individual or group-based activity that mirrors a commitment to the love ethic. Trauma informed knowledge and care are integral to dialogical praxis and involve critical awareness of harm, both for an individual and for an organisation, and a willingness to address this harm (Bloom, 2017). According to Substance Abuse and Mental Health Services Administration (SAMSHA, 2015) this needs to occur without re-traumatising individuals or causing further violence in organisations. SAMSHA identify the practice principles that need upholding as "safety, trustworthiness and transparency, peer support, collaboration and mutuality, empowerment, voice and choice, and [addressing] cultural, historical, and gender issues" (2018, n.p.). This means that the way people or animals or the environment are engaged and how the tasks of addressing issues are pursued, need to reflect the goals of nonviolence, love and ecojustice. Freire writes that "manipulation, sloganising, depositing [knowledge into people], regimentation and prescription cannot be components of revolutionary praxis, precisely because they are components of the praxis of domination" (1970, p. 107).

Transformational change leadership

Anti-oppressive practice (AOP) for the revolutionary social worker involves engaging with conflict, managing high emotions and sometimes addressing threats to safety for individuals, communities and whole ecosystems. Therefore, the decision to undertake practice which goes against the grain of established norms and behaviours in a workplace or community, is not to be done lightly, or alone. Two capacities are focused upon in the love ethic model that are important in planning, undertaking and sustaining justice work to achieve the desired outcome. The first capacity of AOP involves social workers developing transformational change leader/ship (TCL) skills (Ross & Palmer, 2020). The TCL consistently demonstrates the love ethic and employs a collaborative, shared leadership approach between equals. TCL involves love ethic informed skills and capacities which build upon conventional social work skills. Some examples of love ethic informed skills are:

Visioning where an ecological imagination is activated

Pivoting on contradictions, violent spirals and dualisms, turning towards nonviolence

Resisting overt and covert violence

Fostering safe and trauma informed workplaces

Modelling love, nonviolence and ecojustice

Enabling accountability to the low power individual or group as the default position

Leading with love and refusing to hate

Practising love as actions with gentle loving kindness and the willingness to seek justice

Cultivating multiple loyalties and alliances for justice work and

Partnering by co-creating, co-managing and shared decision-making.

The love ethic model recommends three main love ethic informed skills for the TCL team in any situation of violence, lovelessness and eco-injustice. The three skills are:

Challenging with love

Resisting with love, and

Changing with love.

This set of three skills are the main focus in Chapter 3 where examples are provided of how they look in the presented practice scenarios involving interpersonal violence. Additionally, the TCL utilises the specific strategies of: working in groups; building community; employing NVDA to capitalise on people power; seeking a critical understanding of complex issues; and, working nonviolently with conflict and abuses of power.

Group-based spaces for dialogue

The second capacity for dialogical praxis involves using TCL to create relevant group-based spaces to provide the support and people power, and to access the knowledge and resources needed for AOP. AOP uses group work as the main method for engaging and enabling individual empowerment and social group wellbeing and justice. This is because it requires ongoing consideration of the links between the individual, the group and the social context in which the justice issue is located (Brubaker, Garrett, Rivera & Tate, 2011; Singh & Salazar,

2011). To enable group work for dialogical praxis, the 8 step schema provides a guide to engage groups of people where there are significant power differences (Ross, 2020, p. 137). An 'on-the-run' version of the schema is:

Step 1: Prepare yourself and your TCL team - undertake a reconnaissance of the problematics of violence

Step 2: Build relationships with and engage the parties in the ethical concern

Step 3: Form and enable a safe group space by establishing protocols for the group, including a commitment to listening deeply to the parties' views

Step 4: Affirm all positions and interests by being with all parties, while on the side of love and ecojustice

Step 5: Collaboratively establish group agreements relating to the parties' responsibilities in the conflict and the outcomes sought

Step 6: Gather relevant information, research, lived experience stories and place on the dialogue table for consideration

Step 7: Invite reflections on the dialogue process and how people are treating each other. Proactively work to keep the group safe and focused on matters of substance to the low power parties

Step 8: Negotiate fair and substantial justice outcomes. Continue with all steps as needed.

The 8 step schema is a facilitated collaborative process where the TCL team engages low power groups and high power groups in NVDA group-based strategies. The process is similar for individual-with-individual trauma informed practice as the goal includes addressing all types of harm but in particular, moral injury. Moral injury arises when individuals experience unfairness or violence in how they are treated (see next section, Bloom, 2017).

The schema is an adaptation of the collaborative problem-solving approach (Barsky, 2017; McAuliffe, 2014; Conflict Resolution Network, 2019). It also includes the idea of "problem-posing" and combined this approach consists of asking questions about, and seeking solutions to, issues with the people and animals who are being impacted by oppressive (Freire, 1970, p. 65) or traumatic circumstances (Bloom, 2017). Freire calls this approach "conscientizacao" or conscientisation (1970, p. 17) and he places dialogue between equals at the centre of the problem-posing-solving endeavour. Conscientisation involves critical thinking and loving actions to overcome oppression (Freire, 1970, p. 18). It is encapsulated in the term dialogical praxis for present purposes. Justice work involves the impacted parties (people, advocates for animals and the environment) claiming their voice, the right to be heard, and participating in efforts to achieve justice. Therefore, central to TCL is the capacity to engage, encourage and empower people and protect animals and ecosystems. This collective effort can be required for long periods of time when much may be asked of the activists for no immediate return (see for example, Jecks, 2020; Brady, 2020) and no guarantee of success (see, for example, Woodley, 2020).

There are three useful ways to think about how to organise for change and sustain the justice work that is consistent with the love ethic model. These ways are premised on utilising group-based approaches, namely: study circles; communities of practice; and, dialogical communities of practice. Study circles (Brophy, 2001) can be a space for people to share their concerns and learn about the factors influencing the justice concern. Communities of practice (CoP) are groups that form to guide and support justice efforts, self-care, empowerment and trauma informed work. Wenger and Snyder (2000) suggest CoP are potentially radical spaces as they are usually informally organised between peers in workplaces and are therefore not easily controlled by management. In terms of justice work or trauma informed care work, CoP can be peer supervision groups or supported trauma recovery groups respectively. Ross and Palmer (2020) describe the dialogical CoP (DCoP) as a facilitated group where members from low power and high power groups in a conflict situation meet. The purpose is to engage in dialogue as equals to address the issues. The DCoP is a key strategy in the love ethic model.

Trauma informed ideas to create safety

The love ethic model is further refined in this section with ideas and strategies to specifically provide guidance to social workers practising in interpersonal and organisational contexts. A significant influence in this regard is Sandra Bloom who has written extensively on trauma informed care of individuals and trauma informed organisations for addressing violent workplace cultures (Bloom, 2010, 2013, 2017; Bloom & Farragher, 2010, 2013; Bloom & Reichert, 2014). Her work is a good fit with the love ethic model because trauma is indicative of experiences of violence and unfairness. Bloom identifies four types of safety that are needed for trauma informed care of individuals and as well for workers in traumatised workplaces, where:

Physical safety refers to an individual experiencing health, well-being, financial security and being free from violence of all kinds, including self-destructive behaviour

Psychological safety refers to undertaking self-care, self-discipline, self-esteem and self-reflection to live a healthy and productive life

Social safety refers to the ability to interact with others without being compromised or harming others and

Moral safety refers to all actors in a situation or organisation following a set of values and commitments in consistent and respectful ways (2017, pp. 505-506).

Violence can be understood as the threat or experience of unsafety in one or more of these areas and is extended to include all species and the environment. Violence as unsafety occurs where an intrusion against the individual's autonomy is unwelcome or causes loss or degradation. Hem, Gjerberg, Husum and Pedersen use the term "autonomy infringement" (2018, p. 92) to explain this unwelcome intrusion against an individual or group which occurs in situations of coercion and other types of violence. Bloom writes that trauma involves "moral injury" where a "sense of a just world [which] is a critical component of healing" is absent (2017, p. 501). Moral injury starts with any action or failure to act that devalues an individual, usually by someone or an entity who holds power (Bloom, 2017).

This brings a focus to the organisational contexts of social work which can delimit what is possible in neoliberal policy contexts and managerialist workplaces (Pease, Vreugdenhil & Standford, 2018). Bloom explains that many human service organisations are "trauma organised systems" where there is a moral misalignment embedded in everyday interactions and processes (2017, p. 501). Examples of traumatising organisational behaviour are insensitivity and empathic failure, silence and secrecy, injustice and narcissism, authoritarianism, violence and corruption (Bloom, 2017, p. 500).

Social activism within organisations to address these threats to individual and organisational safety can be met with backlash by the power elites. Backlash refers to retaliation and punitive behaviour by high power individuals or groups against challenges to their dominance and privilege. Further, organisations can mirror and reinforce broader societal patterns of inequality and violence (Shier, Nicholas, Graham & Young, 2018). The book explores ways to respond to this complexity of issues by tying an informed, situated understanding of the relationship-sensitive, context-sensitive and power-sensitive dynamics in a situation into the ethical response options.

Securing agreements for accountability

The key elements that can impact the effectiveness of justice work are:

> Willingness to focus on matters of significance to impacted groups

> Substantive and relevant contributions to the issue, especially by high power groups

> Willingness to build sincere relationships and hold relationships over the life of the issue, and

> Attention to, and checking the adverse effects of, high power and low power relations.

Thus, obtaining an agreement from the parties in the conflict to address these elements can provide a basis for holding relevant people accountable (Fox & Miller, 1995). TCL needs to monitor, for example, the extent that sincere relationships are being built particularly by high power individuals. This will manifest in how far they are willing to focus on what the adversely impacted parties believe is significant. Further, the high power members in the dialogue process need to contribute in substantial ways to resolving the issue they have created or failed to address. The practice of obtaining and holding these agreements is likely to be problematic in all three of these agreements and thus, checking the effects of how power is used will be crucial. Relevant steps may need to be taken to shore up a commitment by the parties to show respect and to engage in dialogue without exploitation. The love ethic model and in particular, dialogical praxis, comes into its own in these contested, complex and challenging situations.

Dialogical praxis movements

The ability to do justice work with individuals and groups is influenced by how power is engaged with and understood in the relational, organisational or broader political contexts. Power is the use of direct or indirect influence which can involve a range of actions including persuasion, negotiation, force and violence to obtain certain outcomes (Lukes, 1974). Power is hard to define but its many dimensions and impacts are usually well known from experience for members of low power groups. Young (1990) identifies five faces of oppression, namely; violence, marginalisation, cultural imperialism, powerlessness and exploitation. Lovelessness can be considered a sixth form of oppressive use of power which hooks (2001) explains underpins all other forms of violence. Additionally, eco-injustice needs to be included as an experience of oppression. These seven faces of oppression involve authoritarianism, or anti-dialogue, and a range of other harmful types of power.

TCL employing dialogical praxis and love ethic work more broadly seeks the following movements or changes from anti-dialogue to dialogue:

From violence to nonviolence, resistance and safety

From marginalisation to inclusion, diversity and belonging

From cultural imperialism to decolonisation, cultural humility and reconciliation

From powerlessness to empowerment, power-sharing and addressing privilege

From exploitation to freedom to be and freedom to flourish

From lovelessness to love, compassion and critical understanding and

From eco-injustice to ecojustice.

The book uses the term violence to refer to these types of oppression and includes all species and the natural world in its scope of concern. Attempts by social workers to enable movements from anti-dialogical to dialogical uses of power will be met with conflict, possibly non engagement, backlashes and reactivity. Young's (1990) types of oppression are conceptualised at the social group level which identifies structural patterns of power in an unequal society. AOP also occurs at the direct and interpersonal level where these types of oppression may express in a complex range of ways. The social justice group work literature recommends being aware of micro-aggression which can mirror these broader patterns of oppression (Ortega, 2017). This is related to the idea of parallel process which Bloom (2017) explains as the mirroring of experiences such as trauma that can occur between practitioners and service users.

Love ethic informed work is the basis for AOP where dialogical praxis involves engagements in dialogue between individuals with an interest in the justice issue. The dialogue needs to move beyond discussion and have substantive, relevant material effects to address the justice concern for it to be revolutionary practice.

Conflict negotiation, elegant challenging and resistance

Barsky's (2017, 2019) ideas on how to work ethically in conflict situations are incorporated in the love ethic model to provide more guidance on resisting, challenging and changing interpersonal and organisational violence. Barsky (2017) describes a collaborative conflict resolution process for specific conflict situations which is similar to the useful resources provided by Conflict Resolution Network (2019). It follows a collaborative problem-solving process where there is explicit attention given to the conflict. The parties' interests and positions are identified and any 'in common' interests are used as the basis for negotiating fair outcomes. The love ethic model's 8 step schema encapsulates a conflict negotiation approach premised on a group-based dialogue with an independent facilitator. An integral skill in this conflict work is Thompson's idea of "elegant challenging" (2018, p. 224) which raises issues in a way that allows individuals the best opportunity to hear the issue without becoming defensive or losing face (Matsumoto, 2018).

Ideally, this facilitated group-based problem-solving process creates safety for participants and enables respectful, non blaming discussion and negotiated solutions. It is useful as part of the love ethic model but as a stand-alone process may not be effective if the safety, power and contextual factors are not sufficiently considered. When negotiation and dialogue about an ethical issue is not possible, resistance may be needed. Resistance in organisational contexts refers to nonviolent "practices that challenge management's [or the high power group's] control and attempt to regain autonomy in the workplace [or situation]" (Baines, 2016, p. 127).

To address the limitations of anti-dialogical situations, Barsky (2017) recommends the development of a conflict resolution system. This is a holistic design to build an organisational commitment to working nonviolently and collaboratively with conflict. One aspect of his proposal is the idea of peacebuilding where "rather than merely focusing on ending conflicts, a peacebuilding approach promotes respect, reconciliation, openness, mutual caring and collaboration" (Barsky, 2017, p. 304). Barsky writes that context, power and communication issues related to a conflict need to be considered as part of ethical practice (2019, p. 300). He explains that social workers can promote an ethical organisational culture "by modelling ethical practice and having the moral courage to do what is right even in challenging situations" (Barsky, 2019, p. 188). This is a tall order and the book attempts to provide guidance in this nexus of the individual professional as ethical actor and as an enabler of others in their ethical practice.

Situated ethics and ethics work

The love ethic model incorporates Banks' influential ideas relating to social work ethics (Banks, 2012, 2016; Banks & Gallagher, 2009). Banks explains that ethics "relates to matters of harm and benefit, rights and responsibilities and good and bad qualities of character" (2016, p. 36). In particular, the book aligns with her ideas on how to move from abstract discussions of ethical theories towards a "situated ethics" in complex practice situations to do "ethics work" (Banks, 2016, p. 35). According to Banks (2016) situated ethics refers to locating the ethical concern in its socio-political context. It involves practising with an understanding of ethics as collaborative and contested work and, thereby, as more than the responsibility of an individual practitioner in isolation. Banks describes ethics work as:

> The effort people put into seeing ethically salient aspects of situations, developing themselves as good practitioners, working out the right course of action and justifying who they are and what they have done. (2016, p. 35)

Ethics work is at the centre of the love ethic model and at the micro level of practice the model recommends that social workers adapt the 8 step schema to include relevant aspects of Banks' schema, namely:

Framing work—identifying and focusing on the ethically salient features of a situation; placing oneself and the situations encountered in political and social contexts; negotiating/co-constructing frames with others (including service users and colleagues)

Role work—playing a role in relation to others (advocate, carer, critic); taking a position (partial/impartial; close/distant); negotiating roles; responding to role expectations

Emotion work—being caring, compassionate and empathic; managing emotions; building trust; responding to emotions of others

Identity work—working on one's ethical self; creating an identity as an ethically good professional; negotiating professional identity; maintaining professional integrity

Reason work—making and justifying moral judgements and decisions; deliberation with others ethical evaluations and tactics; working out strategies for ethical action

Relationship work—engaging in dialogue with others; working on relationships through emotion, identity and reason work (dialogue work)

Performance work—making visible aspects of this work to others; demonstrating oneself at work (accountability work). (2016, p. 37)

A loving, anti-oppressive approach to practice has implications for how to interpret Banks' ideas. This is because how the skills are enacted is influenced by how the practitioner understands the power relationships, the context and the contested situation. For example, in an unsafe work situation, it may be part of resistive practice to not declare or make visible aspects of performance work due to the risk of backlash.

The revolutionary social worker needs to ongoingly undertake reflection and analyse processes to grasp the complexities involved and to avoid naïve thinking and acting. Thompson's (2018) schema is useful in this regard and could be placed alongside the 8 step schema and Bank's (2016) schema. Thompson's (2018) schema has three interlinked dimensions which are summarised below, namely:

Personal factors which refer to the influences that are specific to the individuals' biography and circumstances that they can influence

Cultural factors which refer to the dominant views or discourses that may be relevant in how the individuals understand their circumstances and options available them and

Structural factors which encompass enduring broader social patterns of discrimination and inequality that are less directly amenable to the individuals' direct influence in specific situations, where other strategies are needed to challenge these social patterns.

Ross' (2020) work contains an outline of a sophisticated analytical tool (adapted from Bice, Brueckner and Pforr, 2017) that can be utilised as part of the love ethic model. The tool is valuable in situations of complex, intersecting violences where there is conflict involving high power groups and ecological harm. Nevertheless, Thompson's (2018) schema is useful in the micro-contexts of interactions for ensuring the individuals are reading the context (Freire, 1970) and understanding the interlinking relational and power dynamics of these contexts.

Conclusion

The chapter outlined the antecedent influences, key values, ideas, processes and skills of the love ethic model. The love ethic model is a layered and intersecting set of ideas held together in complex practice situations by a conscious commitment to the three eco-values. The eco-values of nonviolence, love and ecojustice provide the moral impetus and guidance to what and who matters in a situation. The eco-values also indicate the type of change that needs to be upheld where: violence is addressed by movements towards nonviolence; lovelessness is addressed by movements towards love; and, eco-injustice is addressed by movements towards ecojustice. These three linked values join with other valued ideas that comprise the key processes of: active participation and voice; accountability and inclusive governance; and, stewardship and sustainability. The main skills of TCL and group-based approaches enable trauma informed, dialogical praxis with parties to collaboratively undertake love ethic work.

For these ideas to be revolutionary they need to be enacted in specific relationships, situations and contexts. Practice which is guided by the love ethic model will be challenging and will require a support base for the TCL team and a developed ability to engage with violence, lovelessness and eco-injustice. To give some guidance about the potential of the revolutionary ideas in practice, the next chapter shows how love ethic work can look in a set of scenarios which assist in contextualising the nature of violence.

Chapter 3

Love ethic work and complexities

The chapter conveys what love ethic informed practice can look like in specific relationships and contexts. It is organised around an inter-linked set of scenarios centring on the relationships between: Sami, a social work student and Kareen, one of her social work lecturers; Sami and Todd, a service user at the Community Support Centre; and, Sami, Kareen and Todd. The scenarios provide a basis for exploring the main components of the love ethic model relevant to interpersonal violence. The chapter also identifies some of the complexities that can arise in practice.

The revolutionary social worker will be constantly asking them-selves and the individuals and groups they are working with – is this love ethic informed practice? The question is answered for present purposes by identifying examples of movements from lovelessness to love, violence to nonviolence and eco-injustice to ecojustice. The movements are presented separately and organised around three different scenario examples. In reality, the movements are not sep-arate and involve the individuals in multiple interplays of situations, relationships and enactments of love ethic informed values, processes and skills. The examples are presented using the three main skills for enacting the love ethic model, namely challenging with love, resisting with love and changing with love.

Each example commences with a summary of the relevant scenario which brings attention to a particular problematic of violence. Some of the scenarios have many problematics of violence which may need consideration by the revolutionary social worker. For example, Sami's experience of domestic violence continues but is not directly focused upon in her interactions with Kareen. Kareen's childhood trauma background continues to influence her relationships, including with students, but is not directly discussed with Sami or with Kareen's professional supervisor. The three examples of love ethic work conclude with reflections on the repeatability and sustainability of the actions and relationships.

Movements from lovelessness to love: Sami and Kareen's relationship

Sami is struggling to do her assessments in the social work course in the context of ongoing risks and distress related to domestic violence. She is recently separated from her partner and lives in temporary emergency housing on a very low income. Her two children are constantly upset and not sleeping at night. Sami became overwhelmed and had a voluntary admission to a mental health hospital where she was secluded after hitting a staff member. Any one of these experiences can have trauma impacts and create mental health issues and disempowerment. All are examples of problematics of violence. Her new partner, Anthony, is very supportive but she is too exhausted to spend any quality time with him. She still feels very ashamed after the hospital experience and seeks solace in her studies. Sami asks for help with the assessment from her social work lecturer, Kareen. She can't focus on her assessment and needs some questions answered before she can get started on it. The appointment with Kareen does not go at all well as she is afforded no empathy or leniency. Instead, Sami is accused of being lazy, which is incorrect, and of expecting Kareen to do her assignment for her – also incorrect.

Kareen has her own challenges stemming from a childhood of domestic violence and powerlessness in trying to help keep her siblings safe. During her early teens, she was impacted by her young friend Amy's sexual assault and felt it was her fault when Amy was expelled from school. Her adult intimate relationships have involved domestic violence and she is being shunned in her workplace. Her colleagues feel she is too opinionated and judges them for 'not walking the talk' of social work. The agony for Kareen is that no amount of privilege afforded by a high status and high paying job, secure housing and no immediate violence in her personal life, spares her from knowing she is not practising what she preaches about love with her students.

She is exceedingly intolerant of students seeking extensions for their assessments, doesn't hesitate to fail students' work to a greater extent than other academics and is reactive if students ask for help with their studies. She avoids thinking about the increasing number of stressed students coming to her office. Several students report Kareen for her unprofessional behaviour. Sami knows them and was tempted to also report Kareen after she left the student consultation meeting with Kareen in tears of frustration and humiliation. Kareen has avoided talking with her professional supervisor about any of this, afraid to open the flood gates and not being able to stop crying.

A specific problematic of violence in Sami and Kareen's relationship started with Sami and some other students who had a bad experience with Kareen. They would meet together over coffee and assassinate Kareen's character, her dress sense, or lack of it, and her poorly organised subject materials. The students' outrage though centred on their criticism of Kareen for teaching about love and acting with seemingly no love in how she treated them. None of the students felt comfortable with what they were doing. Some students were also pressuring Sami to report Kareen for treating her so badly.

Around this time Sami and her friends learn about a loving and empowering group work approach (Brubaker, Garrett, Rivera & Tate, 2011) in one of Kareen's subjects. The students reflect long and hard about the disjuncture between their behaviour and what they were learning. They decide to not keep reporting Kareen and to no longer talk about Kareen behind her back. Instead they will use the group approach and form a University Dialogue Group to empower themselves with their life and study challenges. One day, Sami suggests that they take a risk and invite Kareen to facilitate the meetings for their group as a way of building a connection with her. Kareen is surprised to get the invitation soon after and she accepts. She is a bit surprised to find she is the only academic who has accepted the students' invitation.

In the group space Kareen and the students gradually build a bridge across the lecturer-student divide and have many valuable dialogues. These courageous conversations create a critical understanding of the intersecting challenges in students' and some academics' situations. The word love was not used by any of them to describe their relationship as it was still very unequal outside the group space. Nevertheless, some of the flow-on effects can be seen as examples of movements from lovelessness to love.

Movements from lovelessness to love in Sami and Kareen's relationship are premised on each person being willing to be present for the other, deeply listening to them without agendas and reactivity, and responding with love. It involves a commitment from each person to being self-reflective, open to change towards an equal relationship and understanding the impacting influences in the context. This commitment-into-action aids the uptake of relevant responsibilities by Sami and Kareen and the recognition of how power is being used in the situation. The dual emphasis is on waiting for an invitation to contribute in the other person's life circumstance and showing a willingness to learn with and from the other person.

Challenging with love

Privately, Kareen was challenging herself because she was painfully aware she was falling short of her own love ethic commitment. This was glaringly apparent in students' increasingly angry outbursts in consultation meetings, the formal complaints against her and in the negative feedback in her end of semester teaching evaluations. Kareen had to step up her self-care to be non reactive when in class or in meetings with the students. She finds this exhausting but at least she has stopped adding to the problem of hitting out at students. She has commenced trauma counselling sessions but so far it is more stressful than helpful and she is reluctant to make the link between her personal trauma and what is happening at work. She needs to make amends somehow with the students she had been nothing short of aggressive with and work harder to align her values and practice. Then, unexpectedly, she steps out of her comfort zone with some of her students from the previous semester. They invite her to help them set up and learn how to facilitate their University Dialogue Group.

In the very first meeting, Sami explains why they are pleased Kareen joined due to her inspiring ideas about love in social work. It takes several meetings to build safety and goodwill in the group with the respectful and gentle facilitation by Kareen. The students have not seen Kareen being so comfortable, interested and kind. The topics discussed ranged from immediate assessment matters to family, work and university life. While Kareen was measured in what she contributed, the students put this down to their different roles. During a coffee break, Sami asks Kareen what she finds most challenging about teaching radical ideas such as love in a social work program. They continue the conversation back in the Group. In this safe space, the students raise their observations about how it seems to be one thing to teach ideas and another to actually live them. The relationship and power dynamics shift at this point when Kareen is open with them about her challenges and her regrets for the many loveless actions against students.

At other points, Kareen gently challenges Sami and the other students when they position themselves as victims in discussions about the heavy workload they have, especially when they go on social work placements. They explore how to avoid becoming victims, that is how to avoid becoming disempowered, in their placements. Kareen continues on in the group with students now sharing the facilitation task. During the students' placements she is supportive and gives them guidance on how to negotiate complex situations.

Resisting with love

Sami resisted the harmful impact of the student consultation meeting with Kareen and stayed empowered by debriefing with Anthony. She also followed some old lecture notes which showed her how to consciously pivot on the hurt and turn it into a love opportunity. As a result she took the lead in establishing the University Dialogue Group. Sami chose to not make a formal complaint against Kareen and instead put her effort into creating a safe and loving space with Kareen and the other students. She would wait for the right time to raise her experiences with Kareen who had begun to trust the students with her own challenges.

From early in the Group Sami and the other students felt supported by Kareen but they realised it was an unequal context as soon as they stepped outside the group space. Two of the students will have Kareen as their lecturer next year. For this reason, they bracketed some of the discussions between themselves and had these instead online. Even so, the University Dialogue Group experience had the flow-on effect of helping the students to feel more confident to resist unfair and unloving situations with other academics and their supervisors on placement.

Changing with love

The relationship power dynamic shifted between Kareen and Sami as a result of the University Dialogue Group. Kareen received feedback from the students about how to manage competing responsibilities and pressures when meeting students about their assessments. She gave them some strategies for approaching her and other academics to represent themselves in ways that would be both safe and effective.

Kareen subsequently actively supported Sami in her initiatives at the Community Support Centre even though she thought Sami was too ambitious. Kareen came to recognise the need for more briefing and support of AOP students on field education placements. Alongside this was the need for more support of agencies to provide consistent support to students taking risks so students and other key people in the agency are not scapegoated in any backlash. By the end of Sami's placement, Kareen had acted on this learning by taking the ideas to the social work program meeting for instigating across all similar AOP placements. Kareen steps out of her lecturer role when she joins the Friends of Cows' nonviolent direct action campaigns against an abattoir in the local community. As citizens with shared concerns another space opens up for Sami and Kareen's relationship to be loving towards others.

Are the movements repeatable and thus likely to be sustained?

On the face value of the scenario as presented all these actions are repeatable and may, in fact, build a broader understanding of, and commitment-to-action, for subsequent love ethic work. However, the impact of other power relationship dynamics and the context constraints were not included in the scenario. It remains to be seen whether the relational goodwill and kindness developed between Sami and Kareen and with other students in the group space can be sustained elsewhere.

Kareen can work to foster safe spaces for meeting with students and consider group-based consultations and placement supervisions. Kareen could step up her active support of AOP students, including support to the other students in the University Dialogue Group who experience similar challenges. This could be sustainable if Kareen organises a lecturer peer dialogue group for AOP academics so the university workplace becomes conducive to student-centred and loving AOP.

Movements from violence to nonviolence: Sami and Todd become a partnership, Kareen supports behind the scenes

In her first week of placement at the Community Support Centre, Sami witnesses Todd being bullied by Jack who is one of the Centre staff. Todd was sitting at the lunch table with other service users who attend the Centre each day for recreation, social activities and work experience. Todd was not retaliating as Jack was pinching him and whispering in a menacing tone for Todd to stop it. It wasn't clear to Sami what Todd was doing wrong but it was very disturbing – one, that it was happening and, two, that no one seemed to think it was a problem. Sami makes contact with Todd a day or two later when he is crying and punching the passageway wall. He had been down with the cattle who were corralled for slaughter that day. He was inconsolable. Sami was challenged in trying to connect with him and mostly just stood beside him and listened, without really clearly hearing everything he was saying.

This is an intense time for Todd as he still experiences challenges with anxiety and hearing voices when he is stressed. Todd was referred to the Centre due to the life impacts he faces with early onset schizophrenia. It is believed to have been caused by drug abuse during his teens (McDonald, 2011). He doesn't tell anyone about his mental health condition and finds this the best way to avoid stigma (Thoit, 2016) but at the Centre everyone knows. Some of the staff call him 'schizo' to rile him up and get him into trouble.

Todd loves animals and he attends an equine assistance program (Fine, 2019) on the weekends. He is really skilled at caring for the diary cows and the herd of cattle.

Sami comes to learn that not only Todd but many of the service users at the Community Support Centre were experiencing coercion, bullying and powerlessness. She talks with Todd who seems to be a big influence on the others and gives him support to help them all keep safe. She also helps Todd to keep himself from reacting to things he sees as being unfair and not OK. Todd is increasingly proactive instead of reactive when he is teased by other service users or bullied by Jack.

A particular problematic of violence is precipitated by Sami starting a relaxation group with the service users. It seemed a straightforward idea but she finds they only want to talk about all the issues at the Centre. Todd told her this would happen! She has to shift her plans for the group to meet them 'where they are at'. She gets support behind the scenes to do so with Kareen and other students in the University Dialogue Group. They warn her that management may not be pleased with Sami letting the service users spend the time complaining and to be wary regarding a possible backlash. Some of the service users' families have also become worried about what is happening at the Centre. Unknown to Sami and Todd they have been writing letters of complaint to the Management Committee. Sami does not feel safe to raise the issues with the Centre Manager, Carla. However, with pressure from Todd she decides to call a service user meeting and support them to raise the issues with Carla. Carla is aware of the issues and attends the meeting with Jack for support. She has to get this sorted as the Management Committee are threatening to place her on performance management.

Movements from violence to nonviolence rest on simultaneous movements from lovelessness to love. For problematics of violence to be addressed safe spaces need to be created and relevant individuals need to respond to an invitation to meet about the issue. The meeting space needs to be experienced by people as unwaveringly respectful, loving and focused on relevant matters. The individuals at the meeting need to experience being listened to irrespective of their positionality and views. The inclusion of people who are being impacted by violence brings a level of complexity for the meeting facilitator who needs to stand with the low power individuals while also standing with the high power individuals' being held accountable for harm. This can create reactivity in both groups who will want to have the facilitator side with them against the other group.

The facilitator is to be lovingly present and non reactive towards all members of the meeting and at the same time is on the 'side' of nonviolence, love and justice. This is a high order skill and one that Sami needed to get some briefing for when next at the University Dialogue Group. Kareen was helpful in explaining the micro-level of skills and processes that could assist. Todd and Sami also discussed how the service users would raise their concerns to minimise reactions and blaming. They made a commitment to look for opportunities to strengthen the newly forming relationship with Carla who is also Sami's placement supervisor. Additionally, Todd would try to hold a sense of safety and goodwill in his relationship with Jack. This was going to be a hard call but they were both willing to try to lay some relationship groundwork in the meeting.

Challenging with love

Movements from violence to nonviolence occurred when Sami formed a safe partnership with Todd and when she deeply listened to the concerns of the service users. She finds the relaxation group meetings become almost riotous as Todd and others get outraged about all the unfair and aggressive things happening at the Centre. Sami feels out of her depth and all she knows is that she must listen to them. After that she has no idea and may well be kicked out of her placement. To say she feels challenged is an understatement. Todd tells her about the staff and Management Committee, many of whom she hasn't even met. Sami calls a meeting for the service users to raise their concerns with management. In the meeting, Carla and Jack are supported by Sami to hear the service users. Todd often steps in to help service users say their point calmly and other times he puts forward issues that no one else is willing to say. Carla and Jack are treated with care and respect but feel threatened and placed in a challenging position.

They were challenged in being asked to hear about service users' experiences. Carla and Jack came into the meeting feeling highly defensive but what was disarming for them was how everyone was calm and kind towards them. They could see how Sami's facilitation of the meeting and Todd's support of the service users were the main factors in it going better than they had expected. The service users wanted Carla to make their Centre safer and for Jack to change his behaviour. Carla and Jack explained the pressures they were under with funding and staff cuts and how the Management Committee was asking more and more of them. They stopped short of apologising to the service users for the hurt and lack of safety.

Resisting with love

After the service users' meeting, Jack and Carla subsequently avoid Sami and Todd which Sami experiences as a deliberate marginalising and silencing of her. Carla misses their set supervision meetings. Sami talks with Todd about it but he doesn't mind them leaving him alone. He gets why it is an issue for Sami though as her placement hangs in the balance. Sami gains support from Kareen and her student colleagues in the University Dialogue Group to understand the power dynamics and to keep safe when at the Centre. Sami refuses to accept the backlash that goes on for more than two weeks and with Todd's agreement, she invites Carla and Jack to a debrief meeting. Prior to the meeting Kareen and Sami work to anticipate complexities that might arise. This preparation includes Sami meeting with Carla to explain the purpose of the meeting as being about Sami's learning in such complex situations as the one in which they find themselves.

These preparatory actions helped Sami facilitate a respectful, safe space and to have a courageous conversation (D'Aunno & Heinz, 2017) about how Sami felt she was being treated. The calling of a debrief meeting to directly confront the aftermath of the service users' meeting was in itself an act of resistance. It is also an example of how trauma informed workplaces need to address violence as it happens so it does not compound over time. At the same time, the service users told their families about the meeting and how not much had changed. Some of the staff were being punitive towards service users when Todd and Sami were not around. The families and service users compiled a submission for the national inquiry into the disability sector and when the Community Centre's next accreditation was due they made sure to provide written evidence of the unsafety at the Centre.

Changing with love

Carla, Jack, Todd and Sami were apprehensive about the debrief meeting for different reasons. Jack and Todd had not been to many meetings and they didn't know what to expect. The meeting was intense from the start because of their different experiences, views, roles and authority. The meeting is part of Sami's placement and Carla is one the assessors of Sami's learning. To proceed with the meeting Sami has to move from resisting the backlash to seeking to engage the same people in a dialogue to work through the undeclared conflict. Sami has to be willing to hear what Carla and Jack think of her practice and in turn, they have to be willing to trust the group process and disclose their experiences.

The love ethic model's 8 step schema is followed in part (see Chapter 2) to identify each person's position in relation to the service user meeting. It also is used to explore if there is any common ground of interests in how they understood the meeting, its aftermath and what can be resolved. Sami leads the changing with love by apologising to Carla and Jack for not working more closely with them in calling and running the service users' meeting. Carla takes responsibility by apologising to Sami for not maintaining a supportive relationship with her in the service users' meeting aftermath and acknowledges Sami for initiating the debrief meeting.

Carla informs Sami and Todd about the negative reaction from the Management Committee to the service users' complaints and declares how these complaints had joined up with many complaints from their families. Both Carla and Jack are on performance management programs and are trying to address the issues. The meeting continues longer than expected with Sami and Todd listening more than talking. They take care not to collude with any watering down or covering up of the issues. Nevertheless, it did seem that they each had hold of related parts of a complexity of issues that manifest in lack of care and safety at the Centre. The negotiated solution is to begin by protecting their relationships by creating safety. They each commit to maintain goodwill towards each other and agree that if other issues arise they will seek out each other to discuss it at the earliest opportunity. Further, they agree to meet regularly and to invite a representative of the service users' families to also attend.

Are the movements repeatable and thus likely to be sustained?

Yes, the preparatory work, loving facilitation and courageous conversations strategies could be repeated. For example, the strategies are crucial in Sami's end placement assessment meeting where Carla will review the placement learning with Sami and disclose if she will pass Sami. This is likely to be another intense meeting as Carla explains how she lost face with Sami's challenging questions in the service users' meeting. This is one of many times Sami has been in difficult interactions with Carla which might be regarded as unprofessional practice. Sami listens and shows regard for Carla's experience and apologises for the discomfort Carla felt. Sami then holds some tension by explaining the reasons for her actions. Sami explains how she had hoped that the care and respect shown to her and Jack tempered this discomfort. Carla feels reassured by Sami's response and acknowledges Sami for her leadership and initiative during placement. Sami declares some of the challenges she experienced in not being supported at crucial times by Carla. However, she holds back on the full extent of her abiding sense of moral unsafety.

The answer to the question of repeatability could also be no. While meetings were happening with a focus on the lack of safety at the Centre, the Management Committee continues to avoid taking responsibility. At the very least they need to support staff and provide the necessary resources and training to run the Centre safely. The sustainability of meetings by service users which challenge the staff and management group is very context-specific. It is very much influenced by the willingness of key people in high power positions to stand with and listen to low power individuals or groups. The repeatability of collaborative processes across differences will become harder in workplaces which are not addressing violence in the relationships between staff-staff, services users-staff and management-staff. That is, in the places where violence is impacting across several groups with different complexities, loving change will be much more challenging. But it is possible and external allies can be crucial to support this change. After placement Sami and through her, Kareen and the other students, could maintain a supportive connection with Todd, Carla and Jack and contribute to loving change where possible.

Movements from eco-injustice to ecojustice: Friends of the Cows

The Community Support Centre is the welfare arm of a larger non government agency that operates with a commercial business licence at its adjacent farm. The farm has dairy cows and a small herd of cattle and apples, pears and oranges are grown in the orchards. The farm provides supported work opportunities for many of the service users in the form of voluntary manual labour around the farm paddocks, orchards and buildings. It also involves caring for the new-born calves and packing meat products once the livestock are slaughtered by the mobile butcher service. The business model is regarded as innovative and best practice as it creates work training for people with a disability and is financially viable due to the voluntary apprenticeship model for the majority of the workers.

Early in spring soon after the dairy cows have given birth, the calves are caught and taken into a fenced area away from their mothers. This is standard practice as it ensures the cows keep producing milk for human consumption. This causes much consternation for the volunteer workers but they are told it is just how things are and to get on with it. The calves call out for several days for their mothers, stopping only when being hand fed milk by some of the volunteer workers. The mother cows cry for their babies as they continue to be milked routinely (Bates, 2014).

The drought has impacted the small enterprise which means more of the cattle are to be slaughtered this year. None of the new season calves will be kept but management doesn't tell the volunteers about this plan. The butcher arrives in an enormous truck which is essentially a mobile abattoir.

Todd and the other volunteer workers spend two days herding the cattle marked for slaughter into the holding area. Some of the cattle had been hand reared by Todd and his mates. One in particular is Todd's favourite called Fred. Fred is a Brahman cow with light brown tonings which are darker around his face and upper back. Fred always comes up to Todd when he is putting the hay out for the cattle and nudges. Fred stays close to Todd even though it means Fred misses the best pick of the food. He stands perfectly still while Todd rubs his neck and long soft ears.

The volunteers feel heavy in their hearts the whole time knowing what is planned for the cattle. Todd begs for Fred to be kept longer – he will pay for his feed. However, it is too late because the butcher has already been paid per head of cattle. Also, forward orders for the premium meat products are crucial to keep the Centre viable. Jack and two other paid staff take over the task of helping the butcher and send the volunteer workers back to the Centre to wash up and calm down.

In the Centre the windows and doors are closed during this period, the air conditioner is turned up high even though the temperature is mild and music is allowed to be played as loud as the service users wish. Everybody knows why and nobody mentions what is happening. Todd and several other service users act out their distress by being more boisterous and arguing with staff. Incidents of self-harm and violence between the service users also increases over the following days. Todd is banned for a week at a time from the Centre during most of the spring and early summer. When he is at the Centre he begins to talk with the other service users about how they need to stick up for themselves more and also how they need to try to do something about all the calves and cows being killed. Todd has stopped eating the meat served up each lunch time now he knows where it comes from. Others are copying him and this is being ignored by the Centre's staff as it saves money on the food bill.

The problematics of violence have a dual focus. Todd rallies the service users about the farming of animals by organising a service users' petition. He is also supported by Sami behind the scenes to directly challenge the Community Centre's plan to remove a large to tract of old-growth forest by calling a community meeting.

Movements from eco-injustice to ecojustice are encapsulated in loving and nonviolent responses to lovelessness and violence. Further, ecojustice brings attention to the intersectionalities of unfairness and inequality in relationships between human-human, human-animal and human-natural environment. Equality in relationships is the main focus of movements from eco-injustice where, for example, the killing of farm animals and trees, in terms of the love ethic model, is unethical and should be challenged, resisted and changed. The status quo is organised around inequality between humans, animals and the environment. Thus, there are numerous places to bring love and nonviolence into relationships to work towards ecojustice as the main task of love ethic work.

Challenging with love

Sami finds she needs to act on many fronts over the three months of her placement due to the intersecting types of violence at the Community Centre. In this regard, she comes to highly value the safe relationships with her University Dialogue Group, particularly with Kareen and, as well, with Todd at the Centre. In their own personal time, Sami and Todd challenge the deforestation of farmlands in the rural community by joining a public 'Save the Trees' rally. In turn, there is a backlash against them from the Community Centre as some of the planned tree removals are on the Centres' property. This doesn't stop their activism and they note that the backlash is no longer coming from Carla and Jack, which is some comfort.

Sami and Todd decide more is needed to shift the underlying dynamics of violence at the Community Centre and they increase the challenging with the idea of a community meeting. The challenging with love also involves forming an alliance with the area's Indigenous Elders. First Nation communities around Australia are undertaking a range of sustainable business ideas and land care practices (Harvey, 2016; Perroni, 2019). Additionally, there are other alternatives to animal farming such as growing plant-based products (Fox, 2018; Eswaran, 2018). Such programs could directly benefit the service users and bring in money in a sustainable and positive way. However, ideas which are challenging the way communities and their businesses function are one thing and moving to have them acted on is another. Sami writes a business plan arising from the community meeting and with Carla's help, it is presented to the Management Committee. This action keeps the loving challenge at a heightened level and literally on the Committee's table for many months, beyond Sami's time at the Centre.

Resisting with love

When the Management Committee fails to respond to the business plan, Todd and the other service users increase their nonviolent action. Eventually the butcher refuses to come to the Centre's farm because of all the adverse publicity in the regional newspaper. The service users' media blitz about the harm caused to the workers by abattoirs (Naglesh, 2017) succeeds in creating community outrage. The farm animals are now taken to the local abattoir for slaughter. Many of the service users and their families commence a roadside protest and vigil outside the abattoir. They also refuse to eat Centre meals which use animal products. Todd succeeds in lobbying for the newborn calves to be with their mothers for longer before they are taken to a nearby safe haven farm. Sami has regular contact with Todd and the service users as she has joined their animal activist group, Friends of the Cows, which organises the abattoir vigils. Her professional values and personal values of no harm to all sentient beings results in Sami deciding to become a vegan.

Changing with love

Sami and Todd try to support Carla in the Centre level change effort even though Sami doesn't fully trust her and continues to be afraid Carla will fail her on the placement. Carla is very unsure about the public meeting as she is not convinced anything can be achieved. The dilemma for them all is how to influence the Community Centre's Management Committee without the Committee feeling threatened and being retaliatory. Despite many good ideas at the community meeting, it is not clear how to move from ideas at a meeting to a whole of organisation change. Sami only has time to write a business plan for the Community Centres' Management Committee before the end of her placement.

Some of the fruits of Sami's and Todd's love ethic work come from the determined efforts of the service users and their families who resist and challenge how the Centre treats service users and farm animals. The changing with love pivots on nonviolent direct actions that are feasible and sustainable until there are positive shifts, in this case, with the Centres' Management Committee. This takes time and it is harder for Sami and Kareen to support Carla, Todd and Jack at the agency once Sami leaves her placement.

Are the movements repeatable and thus likely to be sustained?

Yes, the challenging and resisting actions are repeatable despite the risks and challenges involved. For example, in signing a petition, service users were placed in a confronting position, when they were already feeling disempowered and without a voice. The service users trust Todd who trusts Sami who trusts Kareen, but the petition could have caused a backlash. Joining a street march to protest for animal rights is repeatable and also can be effective and less risky if online animal advocacy avenues are used. When individuals in an agency take actions that are challenging of management, these actions are repeatable. To be sustainable though they need internal support and external supporters to avoid the activists being scapegoated or, in Todd's situation, banned from the Centre.

The big idea of trying to change the Community Centre's over-all approach and financial base was, from the start, a big call. When intersecting issues of violence are occurring, it is advisable to take a balcony view of the situation (Ury, 2019). The change work needs a realistic time frame to avoid disillusionment for the protesters. It also requires ready to go strategies to manage the backlash from parties with vested interests in the current arrangement. Eco-activism accounts provide important information about what is needed and how to sustain groups of people in ecojustice struggles. In several examples of eco-activism presented by Ross et al. (2020), the timelines range between one project continuing for more than twenty years and two others continuing for ten years. The projects were, respectively: NVDA to protect local communities from industry pollution (Ross & Puccio, 2020); NVDA to stop development on sensitive public coastal habitats (Jecks, 2020); and, NVDA to stop government infrastructure plans of a highway extension through sacred land and public parkland (Brady, 2020). At the same time, all these long term eco-activist proj-ects have held significant resistance or succeeded in their ecojustice goals.

So, yes, it is possible to sustain loving challenges and to achieve loving change where there is ecological conflict and injustice.

Complexity themes flagged

This section identifies a range of complexities that can be antici-pated in situations of violence, lovelessness and eco-injustice. The scenarios only partly grappled with some of the complexities that will need to be engaged with by the revolutionary social worker. This is due to the focus of the book being on the problematics of interper-sonal violence, where relationships are the main space and resource for the love ethic work.

The complexities are:

The personal and professional is political and as such personal development linked to reflective practice is needed to align the biographical and professional self. This identity work (Banks, 2016) will look different for each person and involves an ongoing commit-ment to self-loving, healing and learning. Healing from trauma and lovelessness experienced as a child can involve a lifetime dedication. Many people join professions such as social work to contribute and make a difference while themselves not knowing safety and love.

The complex power dynamics and interactive nature of contexts is placed central in relationship based love ethic work. This involves framing work and reason work (Banks, 2016) to understand what is needed, done wherever possible in partnership with low power individuals. The arising practice can be confronting, troubling, inspiring, tiring, distressing and conflict-ridden. In addition to the already mentioned components of ethic work, the other aspects are also required, namely emotion work, role work and performance work (Banks, 2016). Underpinning this ethically complex work is the main task of an ongoing commitment to love others and to contribute to their healing and learning.

Ethics work is a social practice where a pure positionality congruent with the love ethic is not always possible. This is because violence, lovelessness and eco-injustice need to be engaged, not avoided or ignored, which can implicate the social worker in compromised situations. It is not possible to act on all fronts that may be required as a lone practitioner. Tactical choices may need to be made about where to focus the challenging, resisting and change actions.

Additionally, ethics as a social practice means that each actor in a situation will have their own ethical sensibility and positionality. The scenarios may have conveyed ethics not only as an individualist practice but also as only a human capacity. Posthumanist writers argue that this view can undermine the interconnection between humans, animals and the environment (Taylor & Pacini-Kerchabaw, 2018). A human bias can also disallow that animals and the environment have agency and contribute to making the world (Taylor, 2013; Haraway, 2015).

The love ethic model requires TCL to be undertaken as a key commitment. However, the revolutionary social worker may be marginalised and undermined if they are trying to influence high power individuals or groups. Thus, their auspice, role and source of authority is influential regarding what is possible in their workplace and beyond.

The revolutionary social worker needs a support base who will stand with them and also 'friends in high places' who will advocate for them and their practice when backlashes occur from privileged individuals and interest groups.

The organisational context of practice intricately influences relationships such that an authoritarian and trauma organised workplace makes creating a loving safe culture and systemic change more difficult. This can impact all workers and service users where even attempts to practice with values such as client-centred practice (Rogers, 1951) and listening to service users' complaints can be perceived as radical and a threat to the status quo.

Collectivising with others to address a violence problematic is central to AOP but also very difficult to do and do well. A key strategy in the love ethic model is group-based meetings with the parties in the justice concern which can be very challenging. Further, respect and constructive dialogue in a well facilitated meeting cannot be assumed to carry over beyond the meeting into instant equality without backlashes.

In community-based situations when economic interests are being questioned and challenged this adds to the complexity of TCL and love ethic work. Attempts to re-orient a welfare agency's financial base or to address ecological conflict need a well organised and supportive network of activist groups using nonviolent direct actions to cultivate people power over long periods of time (Ross et al., 2020). Links with sympathetic workers in key organisations is crucial so activists are not scapegoated when a backlash against the change effort occurs.

The greater the number of interest groups involved or impacted by a change effort, the more extreme the power differences between the groups, the greater the complexity to be engaged.

The harm caused to farm animals, wild animals, the ecosystems and natural environment are not typically part of a social worker's professional work. Therefore, a complexity arises regarding the upholding of the ethical obligation to address the intersecting wicked problems that adversely impact nonhuman species' lives and planetary sustainability. This is because the ethical regard for nonhuman others, which Taylor describes as "more-than-human" (2013, p. 62) relations tends to be located in the personal realm of the social worker as a citizen. The love ethic model extends the scope of ethical concern of social work but this can be challenging to respond to in an ethically congruent and sustainable way. The term "citizen work" can be added to Banks' (2016) ethics work schema to address this otherwise not recognised ethical obligation beyond being a professional in a paid job.

A confounding complexity in love ethic work is the difficulty of enabling interest groups and individuals who have caused harm to take responsibility for addressing that harm. An aspect of this challenge is that privileged, high power and elite groups have an array of mechanisms of power to avoid taking responsibility (Pease, 2010; Ross & Puccio, 2020). One of the most potent mechanisms is blaming the person or group who raises an issue and constructing them as the problem. Failure of high power groups to take responsibility can transgress the rights and interests of impacted parties and can coalesce with other high power groups' agendas to maintain the unjust state of affairs.

Backlashes against people who challenge, resist or try to change the status quo in a situation can take many forms and involve differences of intensity of harm to the people being targeted. Being able to anticipate and negotiate backlashes is a key capacity and has the added complexity that it usually involves resisting some level of personal shunning or criticism. This can hurt and also can lead to what Bloom and Farragher (2013) call negative spirals of reactivity because they argue that hurt people tend to hurt people.

The failure of responsibility, for example, of the management group in a social work agency, to act to uphold occupational health and safety legislation is a legal matter. In this and other situations, it is also a moral matter when the onus to name unsafety issues and to act to have them fairly addressed can fall on the same people who are adversely impacted by management inaction or harmful actions.

Failures of responsibility are underpinned by lovelessness towards the people, animals and environment where the high power individual or group gains from the injustice. Dominant discourses are designed to justify the maintaining of the unjust situations. Any ideas or actions, or failures to act, that devalue or intrude on the autonomy of a person, whole groups of people, animals and the environment are loveless ideas, actions or inactions. This as a value position is contentious and not generally accepted in neoliberal capitalist contexts.

A love ethic model can be corrupted or sold short of its revolutionary potential. Love is not an emotion or positive attitude but an ethic which demands a lot of the TCL social worker and the people with whom they engage. For example, to resist retribution when personally harmed or witnessing others being harmed is one example of what the love ethic demands. To love someone who is causing harm and to avoid treating individuals, social groups or organisations as the enemy or evil is central to nonviolence and justice being both the means and end (purpose) of love ethic work. To love animals is to recognise their equal intrinsic worth to humans and to not abuse or eat them. Each of these are very difficult to do and go against accepted social norms.

Is love enough? It always matters how people act and love should be the lead response as citizens and in social work practice. The love ethic model shows a broad range of ways of thinking about how loving action can look and feel. It may, though, not be enough to keep some people, animals and landscapes safe and sovereign, beyond the revolutionary social worker's sphere of influence. It may not be enough even within their sphere of influence. The witnessing of harm and feeling powerless to stop it happening can be depleting of the hope needed to keep believing in the revolutionary power of love.

In parallel, not causing harm as a social worker is an ongoing ethical obligation and not a straightforward matter. It is especially important for the revolutionary social worker to model nonviolence, love and ecojustice in violent and hopeless engendering situations. This means that the revolution is very personal, embodied, located in time, place and culture, and pivots on each and every thought and action. Significantly, the moral burden is collective as well as individual and personal, not that this should be used as a reason to avoid individual responsibility.

Conclusion: Love is possible in violent relationships

The answer to the lead question of the chapter - has this been love ethic informed practice? - cannot only rely on one perspective, in this instance, mine as the writer. It is for Sami and Todd to say if they came to feel loved and treated fairly and nonviolently in their relationships. For example, for Sami, the person in the non dominant position, in the student role, it is her experience that needs to be foregrounded and listened to as part of Kareen's professional accountability. It is feasible, nevertheless, that the outlined movements could occur and are repeatable and in this sense, the question could be answered in the affirmative. This claim requires some cautions. The constructed scenarios do not include all the influencing factors that are present in real-life situations, including competing accountabilities and loyalties for the social worker. Therefore, the scenarios may imply that love ethic informed actions are more feasible than they are in constrained resource and organisational contexts and in neoliberalist political times.

A highly resilient, dedicated, supported and skilled social worker would be hard-pressed to sustain linked up strategies for change in authoritarian workplaces where they are targeted as a problem by management. (It is possible, though). The idea of a lone hero style of leadership, undertaken to some extent by Sami for love ethic informed AOP, needs unsettling to minimise the loss of committed and talented social workers from places where they are needed most. The recommended TCL approach for implementing the love ethic model is group-based and supported through a network of AOP activists for this reason.

The other main caution is that isolated instances of love ethic work matter but are not sufficient for revolutionary practice for two reasons. The first reason is because revolutionary practice seeks change from dominant groups who are causing harm. The second reason is that revolutionary love ethic work is not an individualist approach to practice. Thus, in the scenarios, it needs to be mainly pitched at the student or service user group level, not isolated relationships with some students or service users. Further, revolutionary practice requires a more concerted strategy by Kareen, in partnership with Sami, Todd and interested others, to support the group-based spaces involving students, service users, and possibly carers and the Centre staff. This collectivist strategy would enable the linking up of individual instances of violence and shared experiences of group members, to empower them collectively to speak up and challenge injustice. The Community Centre Management Committee was not engaged and this became problematic, for example, when they didn't respond to the service users' petition. Less obvious, Kareen's academic peers and managers were absent but it cannot be assumed that their influence on her work was benign. This is important so people who hold some of the responsibility and, perhaps, some of the solutions are not excluded and absolved thereby from the love ethic work.

The flagged complexities show there is unfinished business in exploring how the love ethic model can be further developed. More is needed so the revolutionary social worker can build on instances of love ethic informed practice to enable individuals' and groups' empowerment and voice. Additionally, there is scope to explore the potential afforded by TCL and dialogical praxis where low power and high power groups meet. This requires parties to be willing to engage as equals to be held accountable for addressing trauma and violence.

For now, Chapter 4 draws the values and ideas of the book together so they are liveable for the revolutionary social worker. The chapter includes an evocative visionary narrative to carry the hope of a loving ethic through the micro-complexities of practice whatever form it takes.

Chapter 4

A new beginning: Being revolutionary love

The last chapter locates the potential of the love ethic model in the specificities of our respective personhoods and life experiences. This is necessary because ideas alone do not have revolutionary power, even though perhaps they hold the promise of it. Ideas need to be lived and consciously used and adapted to guide that living. If I am not willing to practice living the ideas I write about here, the integrity of the project falters. This need not be a perfect project to be revolutionary. A number of final reflections are presented that place us in a relationship going forward and place both of us with our kin so we may never feel alone, as in on our own, in the revolutionary work. The chapter is an invitation to you to take away with you anything that might be of value to you in your life and work, possibly even your life work. Beyond the usefulness or otherwise of the book, the chapter concludes with a call to social workers to practice right here, right now, being revolutionary love.

Gathering some threads together

There is a rich tradition of anti-oppressive theories and practices which are consistent with the love ethic model that are duly acknowledged here. The book stands in this tradition and places a focus on values to live by precisely because values are cherished beliefs. Compared with abstract ideas in a book, the values already 'belong' to the individual. hooks describes this as "living with the truth of [...][our]

values" (2000a, p. 90). I have endeavoured to convey how the identified values derive from my life and work experiences and influence my practice, in this moment, the practice of writing. The book suggests that a set of values under the umbrella of the eco-values of nonviolence, love and ecojustice are the key heart ingredients for living in a revolutionary way. There is a wide path for everyone to contribute to the nonviolent, loving and just revolution that is already underway. This is because the invitation stands for any one to undergo a conversion in their life from the ethic of domination to an ethic of love (hooks, 2000a). hooks explains that the "space of lack [of love] [...] is also the space of possibility" (2000a, p. 221).

In turn, ethics is a social practice, not ever done on my own as I am always practising in relationship with others. Thus, the offerings in the book are the result of my learning from all the relationships I have experienced. The offerings are also the result of all the ways of knowing and being of the other individual humans, animals and nature entities who have joined with me in these relationships. I am therefore, and you are too, already practising how to be revolutionary love, even as you may not agree with me or even use the same language. I suspect though, that our values are similar and where different we could be enriched in the sharing of these differences. It is the case that every day and night, I need to be aware of how I am being in the world of relationships. I also need to be willing to pivot on experiences of violence, lovelessness and eco-injustice, including by my own hands, to nonviolence, love and ecojustice. This willingness to learn and then to pivot is made possible, for me, by an unshakeable belief in the healing and transformational power of love. The thousands of people I have met, across the social worker-service user divide and the social work academic-student divide, have shown me both what love is and how it really matters that I am loving towards them. This is one part of the source of an unshakeable belief in love.

The other part of the source of an abiding belief in, and knowing love, is the experience of the life force of nature in all her beauty, resilience and sustenance. Haraway argues:

> No species, not even our own arrogant one pretending to be good individuals in so-called modern Western scripts, acts alone; assemblages of organic species and of abiotic actors make history, the evolutionary kind and the other kinds too. (2015, p. 159)

This locates us as members of the human species in relationship with all our kin, for the purpose of making liveable worlds with other species and nature (Haraway, 2015). Taylor explains this requires a common world's ethics that involves the "co-creating of de-colonised more-than-human framings of how to be in [a] relationship" (2013, p. 62). In turn, this allows an emphasising of the spirituality or non materiality of individuals, groups and entities who are our kin. Martin writes that thereby "you no longer know yourself as a 'person', you've become an Entity amongst other Entities. Through a relational ontology, the connections are restored, relatedness reciprocated and maintained" (2003, p. 207).

One implication is that I, you, all of us, belong to a web of life which has a diversity of agency and wisdom. This can help ease the weight of an individual sense of morality, but not to avoid our proper responsibilities, as we contribute our part. This is important for a number of reasons but the main reason is that we perhaps need to be assured at times that we are doing enough where we are and with whom we are in relationship. If on truthful self-reflection, this is not the case and we could do more, there will be a way of contributing where we are which at the same time affirms who we are. West explains that the turning of our soul away from violence in all its forms is "done through one's own affirmation of one's worth – an affirmation fuelled by the concern of others" (cited in hooks, 2000a, p. 94). The revolution is not separate from us and has not left us behind, it can be joined at any time by the smallest act of love, including love of ourselves.

The love ethic model is offered as a loving, critical posthumanist ecological imagination, framework and grouping of values, processes, strategies and skills that can guide the revolutionary social worker. In different ways critical posthumanist, eco-feminist and Aboriginal world views agree that a trans species ethics is needed. Trans species ethics acknowledges all animals' and entities' spirituality, agency and ability to experience pain and compassion (Willett, 2014; Ross, et al., forthcoming). Posthumanism is not beyond the human or anti the human.Rather it is a recognition that humans have always been an integral part of, not separate from or superior to, nature and the web of life and relationships this entails. Haraway conveys a sense of what this means when she writes "I am a compost-ist, not a posthuman-ist: we are all compost, not posthuman" (2015, p. 161). Nevertheless, Braidotti argues that the human influence on nature is so substantial it is impacting the geography on the planet, climate and diversity of life (2013, p. 5).

Planetary pivoting is underway

The book necessarily focuses on violence and the harm caused by it. However, the focus can obscure and inadvertently downplay the pervasiveness of a commitment to nonviolence, love and ecojustice, in its many forms and places. It is this pervasiveness of commitment by tens of millions of people across the planet, our trans species relatives and other sentient beings that is the precious resource the book seeks to tap into and further encourage. When loving beings witness violence it can result in a range of feelings and responses, including outrage. If outrage motivates revenge and retaliation, it is not love. Outrage which springs from love is the pivot point for personal and planetary revolutions.

Another way of saying this is that outrage against violence and injustice is understandable and part of the momentum required for love ethic work. As Freire (1970) writes, though, the outrage needs tempering to avoid naïve thinking and actions that can add to the harm. The love ethic provides that tempering and implies that there is no enemy. Rather, there are people who are causing harm who need to be accountable for that harm. The other important premise of the love ethic model is that nonviolence, love and ecojustice are the values and methods for achieving this accountability. As well, and interrelatedly, the revolutionary social worker, inspired by the love ethic model, offers loving regard to the people, animals and landscapes who are harmed and to the people who need to address that harm.

Between these two ethical positions – love matters and there is no enemy – is the need to challenge the co-existence of violence and love in relationships and situations as an acceptable social norm. hooks (2000a) argues that if there is violence occurring this is not love. Nevertheless, people and animals can experience a mix of love and violence in the same relationships. The significance is that the potentiality for loving responses is to be found in the full spectrum of human and animal experiences, including in violent situations. There are pivot points to turn from violence to nonviolence, to model this in our lives and work and to resist retaliatory actions.

Peavey (2000) claims that justice can be achieved through empathy, nonviolence, cooperation and person-to-person contact. She elaborates further:

> There is a great difference (though often a fine line) between working from the heart and manipulating people by appealing

to their emotions [....]. Heart politics [...] is about making a deep connection with the life found in a specific place, culture or area of land. Since connection is with life, it is inconceivable to think in terms of organising to kill, to punish, or to destroy. To use love of people for deadly ends is immoral and crazy as well as inconsistent. (2000, p. 1)

The following poetic was written in the early 2000s (Ross, 2002) in an attempt to convey the ethical challenges of that epoch. It depicts a myriad of situations which were reported in the media at the time, or encapsulate experiences I was aware of, or by which I was impacted. The poetic remains relevant almost 20 years later.

Interconnectedness of life-love and death-violence

Our bodies are our homes, our weapons of defence and our tools for change -
All forms of life have equal intrinsic worth

All forms of violence do harm.

We are of the one planetary life heartbeat -
I am the decaying body in the disused storm water drain
My grandfather is the paralytic body after another bottle of cheap wine
You are the sea of bodies from an oil spill in a world heritage area
My clients are the institutionalised group of grey bodies, glazed eyes fixed on TV screens
A workmate's child is the young body leaking life after a laced shot of heroin
Our child is the rigid, uniformed body force fed the three Rs
Your sister is the drug induced, sterilised body cut into to the rescue a child born into poverty
I am the infected body isolated and outcast
A man who looks like my father is the hysterical male body who staggers over the war zone border
His brother in law is the fatherless body unable to father his own child

I am the pod of beached bodies, no will to live
A student's parent is the invisible black body, no land, no citizenship

Your nephew is the motionless body, no work, no money.

We are all interconnected
I am the body. You are the body. Animals are the body. Nature is the body
Basic human, animal and environmental rights & wellbeing must be defended
Wherever possible
With great collective intelligence
Love
Nonviolence
And justice -
Women have a right to culturally appropriate, safe, supportive births with minimal technological intervention
All people have an inalienable right to their homelands and to live in peace
All children have a right to be loved and valued by at least one other person as they grow up
All people have a right to food, water and shelter and non exploitative love
All people have a right to defend themselves nonviolently but not to kill others or take up weapons of mass destruction
The environment and animals of the planet have a right to exist without exploitation.
We are all collectively but differently responsible
Some people are better positioned and resourced to make a difference than others
I cannot be free
While you are imprisoned.
You cannot be free

While I remain silent.

We are all capable of acting as moral beings, are already moral beings -

The infected body alone and outcast. I talk with my child about the harm her words can cause in the school yard

The hysterical male body staggers over the war zone border. My friend applies to be a volunteer with CARE Australia

The fatherless body unable to father his own child. My feminist colleagues teach social work students of the need for our theorising to be inclusive and for their practice to respond to the complexity of trans-identity and trans-species difference and suffering

The white body dripping with gold and American dollars travels the world for free. His wife chooses to work in a devalued profession to make a difference in her community

The screaming body grasps at a starving corpse as the sun beats down. Neighbours who have known hunger as children, give a large donation to Community Aid Abroad

The deeply horrified body continues to bear arms against friends and neighbours. His son and their sons are part of the mass of people who pull down the Berlin wall

The pod of beached bodies, no will to live. Locals swing into Operation Save the Dolphins action and share their knowledge with other coastal towns

The nation body in peril due to foreign debt and unchecked imperialism. Its people ensure they have food for their children by refusing to export essential needs to imperialist countries

The female body raped and dumped. Mens' groups become proactive in challenging their male friends' and male neighbours' violence

Wars and violence are not inevitable and inherent characteristics of human societies.

Rage, hatred, pain, alienation, fear, resentment and revenge are not healed or changed by more rage, hatred, pain, alienation, fear, resentment and revenge

Strategic resistance and nonviolent direct actions for peace and justice

Do make a difference

Hope, love, respect, compassion, forgiveness, courage, nonviolence, understanding, confidence, persistence

Can and do heal sentient beings and change violent situations.

Invitations to pivot towards love

The contributors in this segment offer invitations to pivot from lovelessness to love by calling on non material wisdom, trans species learning and empathy to foster bonds between humans, animals and nature. This is about cultivating an ecological imagination (Thomashow, 2014) and heart. Thich Nhat Hahn's writing conveys the significance of the interconnectedness and interdependence of sentient beings as one with nature:

> We have to look deeply at things in order to see. When a swimmer enjoys the clear water of the river, he or she should be able to be the river [...]. If we want to continue to enjoy our rivers – to swim in them, walk beside them, even drink their water – we have to adopt a non-dual perspective. We have to meditate on being the river so that we can experience within ourselves the hopes and fears of the river. If we cannot feel the rivers, the mountains, the air, the animals and other people from their perspective, the river will die and we will lose our chance for peace. (1991, pp. 104-105)

The invitation is to pivot towards being 'at one' or in kinship with rivers, trees, mountains, sky, ocean.

Starhawk describes the urgency to dream and live a new way of being:

> Our ultimate interests are the same – restoring a sense of sacred to the world, and so restoring value to our own lives and to the community of beings – human, plant and animal – that share life with us.

> Still some of us have not yet lost hope.

> That hope sways on an edge so delicate that it is possible that the choices any one of us makes could tip the balance [...]. And perhaps it is you, your reaching, your voice, your work, your joy, your love, that will make the difference [...]. Or perhaps it is up to all of us, to join our hands, our voices, to reach into the dark and reshape it into a clear night sky where we can walk without fear

83

into a well of healing from which we can all drink [...].

For that force pushes us towards each other, flesh to flesh, heart to heart – that moves us to dance, to work, to birth and to weave – is a power that never stops reaching out for life.

The night, the moment, each moment presents us with a chance to meet that power, to gasp it, to dream it into being.

It is in your eyes.

It is in your hands. (1988, pp. 181-182)

The invitation is to pivot towards holding hands, hooves, paws, wings and tentacles with other species to co-create a common liveable world.

The following excerpt from a TedTalk by Simard (2016) conveys that there is much humans do not know. She suggests that perhaps we care not to know about the life force of trees for what may then be asked of us. Her scientific research over many years using radioactive trace substances placed into trees provides a glimpse of how trees communicate and support each other. Simard talks at length about the nature of underground microscopic organisms and nutrients. The organisms create networks of complex transfers of substances and messages between the trees near each other. This in itself is fascinating and alerts humans to tread carefully literally around trees. Simard's research asks us to appreciate that just because we can't see something happening is not to assume nothing is happening.

How trees talk to each other

[...] The evidence was clear.

The C-13 and C-14 was showing me

that paper birch and Douglas fir were in a lively two-way conversation.

It turns out at that time of the year,

in the summer,

that birch was sending more carbon to fir than fir was sending back to birch, especially when the fir was shaded.

And then in later experiments, we found the opposite,

that fir was sending more carbon to birch than birch was sending to fir,

and this was because the fir was still growing while the birch was leafless.

So it turns out the two species were interdependent,

like yin and yang.

How were paper birch and Douglas fir communicating?

Well, it turns out they were conversing not only in the language of carbon

but also nitrogen and phosphorus

and water and defence signals and chemicals and hormones --

information.

[…] This below ground mutualistic symbiosis called a mycorrhiza

was involved […]

[which] connects different individuals in the forest,

individuals not only of the same species but between species, like birch and fir,

and it works kind of like the Internet […]

[Simard outlines a detailed picture of how the networks work and continues]

The young seedlings […] have established within the network

of the old mother trees.

In a single forest, a mother tree can be connected to hundreds of other trees.

And using our isotope tracers,

we have found that mother trees

will send their excess carbon through the mycorrhizal network

to the understory seedlings,

and we've associated this with increased seedling survival

by four times.

Now, we know we all favour our own children,

and I wondered, could Douglas fir recognise its own kin [...]

So we set about an experiment,

and we grew mother trees with kin and stranger's seedlings.

And it turns out they do recognise their kin.

Mother trees colonize their kin with bigger mycorrhizal networks.

They send them more carbon below ground.

They even reduce their own root competition

to make elbow room for their kids.

When mother trees are injured or dying,

they also send messages of wisdom on to the next generation of seedlings.

So we've used isotope tracing

to trace carbon moving from an injured mother tree

down her trunk into the mycorrhizal network

and into her neighbouring seedlings,

not only carbon but also defence signals.

And these two compounds

have increased the resistance of those seedlings to future stresses.

So trees talk. (See Simard's full TedTalk, 2016)

The invitation is to pivot towards stewardship of old growth forests and wild landscapes as a moral baseline to protect nature's ability to sustain life.

An implication of the love ethic model and these perspectives is that loving trans species ethics that extend ways of understanding and being need to be cultivated by humans. Willett identifies four aspects of what she calls "trans species communitarianism" (2014, p. 21) that can guide human and nonhuman relationships. The first way humans can expand our understanding and relating is the idea of "subjectless sociality" which unlinks relationship from identity and other subject categories. This makes possible the appreciation of trans species shared experiences such as similar fear responses when a large scale bushfire rages through shared human and animal communities. Another example that I have experienced, is the mournful sounds that emanate from the killing fields soon after a forest is clear felled. Willett's (2014) second idea is "intersubjective attunement" where humans consciously adjust our behaviour to respond to the needs of animals or nature. These trans species ethical sensibilities enable an appreciation of shared experiences of "affect clouds of biosocial networks [...] [which are] not properties or states interior to bound subjects or nonporous bodies" (Willett, 2014, p. 17). The biosocial network can be thought of as a home and common shared experiences across species differences. Humans and animals playing and enjoying each others' company or helping each other would be examples of this biosocial shared world. Willett's fourth trans species ethic involves humans recognising animals' spirituality and their sense-making and ability to express compassion and other feelings (2014, p. 18).

A short-hand way of grasping Willett's (2014) trans species communitarian ethical skills is the idea of empathy being extended to include more of our human kin and as well to include nonhuman animals, that is all of nature in all forms of materiality and spirituality.

Full circle: The personal and professional is political

The book draws to a close where it started and thus brings us full circle. The personal and professional is political in more senses than perhaps even an ecological imagination can reveal to us. Our values are part of what makes up our sense of ourselves and claims to be good people. However, love ethic informed interpretations of values suggest that a professed love, for example, of animals is not a love of animals unless it is acted upon. Incongruence between our values and how we live our lives is one crucial way our ethical integrity is compromised. The individual actions of each of us have a collective impact that constructs a politicisation of who is valued and who is not, who eats whatever they wish and who is eaten, who is free to move within and across national boundaries and who is an illegal immigrant and placed in off-shore detention, who is worthy of welfare payments in a pandemic and who is not.

The following poetic conveys how this politicisation occurs through violence against unloved low power individuals and groups with tacit support by society.

I love my family

I love my family. Now that I think of it we do move around a lot, never in any one place for too long. I hear mum and dad talking about what will happen if they find us. It makes me think maybe we're not meant to be here. That they will find us and take us back to where we came from. Mum and dad don't like to talk about where we came from, I'm too young to remember what happened. But we must have fled. Home must not have been safe. But I'm safe now. Safe and happy with my family, always going on adventures.

One day, I heard the dogs barking. The barking got closer and closer, until we were running for our lives. Scared, scared, I'm so scared. We say nothing as we run together, my family and I.

But it's no use. They got to us. They rounded us up, surrounded us whole while we screamed. They marched us out from the bush and into a clearing where we were herded into a truck which was dark and cold. There was a tiny gap in the side of the truck, I watched in fear as the trees turned to houses turned to buildings as we were taken far away from our home.

My parents stand close to me, to us. We say nothing. Fear in our throats. I'm at the back of the truck and they all stand in protection in front of me. We drive for hours, over hills and through towns. I'm so tired I can barely stand up.

The truck slows and my family freeze in horror. My dad says he can smell something out there. He starts to pace frantically.

There is blinding bright light as the truck doors are thrown open and we are herded out to meet our reckoning.

Is this our punishment for leaving the place we originally came from? Somewhere so cruel and dangerous that we couldn't lead a happy, safe life.

I'm last in line as we come out from the truck. There are people everywhere, staring at us. A large building looms ahead and we are rushed into it.

Mum and dad scream as they are torn apart. I scream as I am separated from them.

One story line is...

Up ahead the other cows scream as they are corralled into their death chamber. The ground turns red, covered in their blood. I walk on the blood of my family as I am prodded and shoved to meet the same fate.

I'd give anything to be back in the bush, looking for food with my family.

A call to practice being revolutionary love

On behalf of the millions of animals who are killed every day across the world, I invite you to act with love to stop this extreme level of violence. The first step involves extending the empathy you feel for the people you love, your family pets and favorite wild animals to include all other animals. Other loving and nonviolent steps will then become clear and possible (Francione, 2016).

Another story line and invitation...

On behalf of the hundreds of thousands of asylum seekers who are displaced, held in camps, imprisoned in off-shore detention centres and denied their basic human right to seek refuge, I invite you to act to stop this extreme level of lovelessness.

The book is premised on an ethical stance that revolutionary practice is "love in action [...] [that is,] we must [...] actualise love [...] [and] see love as a practice" (hooks, 2000a, p. 165). Kelly and Westoby write that the energy for this love ethic work comes from "soul force" which is expressed through the "art and practice of gentling" (2018, p. 182). Gentling or the cultivation of gentleness is a timely idea as you prepare to finish the book that can place a considerable moral pressure on you. Kelly and Westoby argue that we can inadvertently "perpetuate violence when we push a certain ideology onto people [...] it may be done in the name of nonviolence – but it is this unconsciousness that makes it endemic and colonising in nature" (2018, p. 172). I wish therefore, to unsettle my claims and passions that are this book and concur with their suggestion that:

> The gift of gentling is to put 'truth' to work [...] [where] the more that truth is disarmed and free of any trace of intentions to dominate or colonise, the more the intellectual and moral force of truth can become the free spirit that is the heartbeat of change. (Kelly & Westoby, 2018, p. 172)

So let me gently ask of you, to feel free to take anything or nothing from the book as you wish. Also, please don't let the moral imperatives in the book impose on your way of being, rather may you feel we are partners in making a contribution already, even before you read the book.

Finally, I have one last invitation for you to consider. Would you like to practice being revolutionary love with me and millions of other people, or more accurately, continue being revolutionary love?

You don't need to graduate to be a revolutionary social worker.

You can be a revolutionary (social worker as a) psychologist, nurse, lawyer, fitness trainer, restaurant worker, labourer, volunteer, parent, child, animal. Nature is already revolutionary love.

You can be a revolutionary (social worker as a) citizen and an asylum seeker as Behrouz Boochani (2018) has so powerfully shown us.

You can start wherever you are, right here, right now.

By acting with love you will be immediately part of the revolution.

Thank you.

Farewell,

Dyann

Glossary

Accountability – taking responsibility for impact of actions and failure to act – see responsibility

Active participation – individuals and groups being proactive in contributing to matters of importance to them – see responsibility, inclusive governance, voice

Agency – the ability of individuals and groups to act in their own best interests – see empowerment

Agreements – informally negotiated warrants identifying principles, strategies and goals for achieving nonviolence, love and ecojustice

Animal rights – all nonhuman animals being afforded equal intrinsic worth by humans which enables respect for their rights: to be, to live and to experience freedom and love

Anthropocentric harm – the full spectrum of violence, lovelessness and injustice caused by human privilege and superiority (Eaglehawk, 2020) – see human-centrism, speciesism

Anthropocentrism – human animal bias against nonhuman animals resulting in a lesser valuing of their lives, feelings and contribution to life on the planet

Anti-dialogue – authoritarian control and imposition of will on low power individuals and groups – see managerialism, oppression

Anti-oppressive practice – movements towards nonviolence, love and ecojustice – see revolutionary practice, love ethic work, group-based strategies, community work

Anti-oppressive theories – for example, anti-racism (critical race, whiteness theories), postcolonialism, critical theory, feminism, minority group standpoint theory, ecofeminism, love ethic, post-humanism, Indigenous ideas, veganism. Ideas which enable the challenging of an ethic of domination and its stigmatising and harmful impacts on individuals and groups

Anti-racism (critical race, whiteness theories) – ideas which critique the dominant racial group with Anglo-Saxon heritage and its colonisation of First Nation People and lands. Challenges racial superiority and privilege which has caused displacement, genocide, stolen lands, forced removal of children and systemic racism in settler societies

Autonomy infringement – actions or situations which are unwelcome and impose upon an individual's or low power group's safety and freedom

Backlash - forms of retaliation and punitive behaviour which, by intention, or by failing to stop subsequent harm, enable high power individuals or groups to reassert their privilege and dominance over others

Being present (in love) – the space of purposefully offering self in relationship where fully conscious and open-hearted. Can include invitations to engage in dialogue and to change

Bodily autonomy – the experience of safety, wellbeing and freedom as an individual human, animal or landscape

Challenging with love – holding a loving regard for the high power individual or group while inviting them to change their ideas and actions

Changing with love – holding a loving regard while standing with and supporting movements towards nonviolence and ecojustice

Coercion - situations where force is used against an individual or group. The force can be legally sanctioned and can also take the form of threats and direct use of force. Coercion exists when a less restrictive option is not used in professional contexts

Communities of practice – purposeful groups for practising community work within an equal group which can become a support group during justice work – see group-based strategies, social action, empowerment, community work

Community work – the use of group-based strategies to address the social and community level of violence, lovelessness and eco-injustice – see anti-oppressive practice, love ethic work

Conflict negotiation – a set of ethics, skills and processes which seek to engage parties in the conflict in its resolution or negotiated trade-offs – see eight step schema for justice work, transformational change leadership, dialogue, dialogical praxis, conscientisation

Conscientisation – group-based education and empowerment processes for low power individuals to critically understand the justice issue and to undertake action to address it (Freire, 1970) – see critical understanding, critical acting

Context – the socio-cultural, economic, environmental and political milieu or setting of the individual or group. Also can refer to locations such as organisations, workplaces and communities

Context-sensitive – being aware of the nature of the context and being responsive to its influence when engaging with an individual or group

Critical acting – the ability to undertake appropriate loving actions that cause no harm and can progress love ethic work

Critical social work – a range of approaches to social work that hold a lens to the nature of inequality and other forms of oppression. Includes the obligation to be critically self reflective regarding own use of power – see anti-oppressive theories, feminism, anti-racism

Critical thinking – the ability to understand the context and power dynamics in a justice issue and to discern the appropriate loving actions required in a situation

Critical understanding – the ability to make meaning from critical thinking and acting 'in situ' that encompasses the experiences and knowledge of the relevant parties. This involves political analysis and knowing how to interpret the impact of violence, lovelessness and eco-injustice in specific situations

Cultural humility – the willingness to learn from a different social or species group their ways and values and to respect and honour without exploitation or presuming to know best for them

Cultural imperialism – the presumption of knowing best for a different social or species group while appropriating or exploiting the group for the high power individual's or group's advantage

Decolonisation – actions undertaken by members of dominant racial groups to avoid and undo the harm caused by racism, to negotiate compensation and seek reconciliation. Involves the dismantling of systemic racism, the inclusion of First Nation People in national constitutions and includes return of sovereignty and land rights

Dialogue – the meeting of low power and high power individuals as equals to engage in non exploitative discussions and problem-solving on matters of violence, lovelessness and eco-injustice

Dialogical praxis – utilising transformational change leadership, the love ethic, skills and strategies to enable dialogue in specific situations, drawing on recurring cycles of critical thinking and acting in a facilitated collaborative group-based setting – see transformational change leadership, eight step schema for justice work, love ethic model

Disadvantage – the effects of discrimination on individuals and groups

Discrimination – acts, including failures to act, which are harmful, e.g. exclusion, racism, speciesism

Duty of anti-discrimination – a recommended ethico-legal principle relating to the responsibility to address discrimination which is typically experienced as stigma and disadvantage for low power individuals and groups – see safety, nonviolence, ecojustice

Duty of care – an ethico-legal principle that refers to the obligation of a practitioner to act in the interests of the service user, where the decision to not act needs to also be in their interests. A love ethic informed approach requires the practitioner to be alert to abuses of power that cause harm to the service user under the veil of duty of care

Duty of confidentiality – an ethico-legal principle that requires the practitioner to protect the privacy of the service user and to only disclose relevant information to third parties with the individual's consent. A love ethic informed approach requires the practitioner to be alert to abuses of power that cause harm to the service user under the veil of confidentiality

Duty of ecojustice – a recommended ethico-legal principle that refers to any actions which seek to enable ecojustice in a specific situation

Duty of environmental precautionary principle – a recommended ethico-legal principle in professional practice that requires a for-caring for the sustainability of the environment – see environmental precautionary principle

(Duty of) informed consent – the ethico-legal principle of requiring a practitioner to ensure the individual or group understands what they are agreeing to when seeking a service, resource, signing a document or participating in research. This must occur without direct or implied coercion

Duty of nonhuman animals precautionary principle - a recommended ethico-legal principle in professional practice that requires a for-caring for the wellbeing and justice of nonhuman animals – see nonhuman animals precautionary principle

Duty of non-maleficence – a recommended ethico-legal principle that is embedded in all the ethico-legal principles as the baseline responsibility in professional practice. It requires the avoidance of harm and addressing any harm that may occur – see non-maleficence, nonviolence

Duty of procedural justice – an ethico-legal principle that requires fairness in processes, and relationships and for the individual or group to be fairly heard – see social justice, species justice, environmental justice

Duty of social precautionary principle – a recommended ethico-legal principle in professional practice that requires the for-caring of the wellbeing and justice of people – see social precautionary principle

Duty to avoid negligence – an ethico-legal principle which can be claimed by, or on behalf of an individual or group, who was owed a duty of care where a dereliction of this duty has occurred. A love ethic informed approach goes further and obliges the practitioner to be proactive in addressing harm and taking appropriate responsibility for any dereliction of their duty

Duty to love people, animals and nature – a recommended ethico-legal principle which provides the motivation to uphold all others. The individuals who are engaged in professional situations can expect to feel they are treated with compassion, understanding, nonviolence and justice. High power individuals and groups can also expect to experience love with resistance, challenge and invitations to change behaviours which are experienced as harmful by others

Duty to warn – an ethico-legal principle which requires the practitioner to act to inform a third party if the service user makes threats against their safety. A love ethic informed approach requires that the practitioner is alert to abuses of power that cause harm to the service user where they may need to be warned about the potential harm of receiving the service

Eco-feminism – theories which make the link between oppression of women and the oppression of nature where human-on-human inequality is mirrored in human-on-nonhuman animal inequality and the privileging of human-made artefacts, as per cultural products, at the expense of nature-made

Ecojustice (ecological justice) – encompasses human/social justice, species justice and environmental justice and movements towards any or all of these

Eco-injustice – the absence of experiences of fairness for humans, nonhumans and the environment – see violence, harm, trauma, love-lessness

Ecological conflict – multidimensional and multi-parties disagreements about the use of the environment in some individuals' and groups' interests, at the cost of others' interests and the sustainability of the environment

Ecological imagination - the ability to think and envision in loving, critical, creative and ecologically informed ways that recognise the interconnectedness and life force of the planet

Economic sustainability – a social system of production and exchange of goods and services that respects and protects the environment, and disallows extreme wealth based on human and species exploitation and environment degradation

Eco-social work – love ethic informed activism and emergent theorising that seeks to uphold the highest expression possible of the public interest

Eco-values – the interlinked values of nonviolence, love and ecojustice which comprise the main values of the love ethic

Eight step schema for justice work – a component of the love ethic model for guiding transformational change leaders in enabling dialogue to address harm

Elegant challenging – raising an issue in a way that avoids loss of face for the individual or group, yet holds them to their appropriate responsibility

Empowerment – the ability to act in own or others' best interests with others, using eco-values and the love ethic model

Environment – refers to nature, ecosystems, specific landscapes or broad sense of a country's or the world's natural systems of life. It includes humans, nonhumans, non-sentient beings and the spirituality and materiality of the planet

Environmental justice - the individual part of an ecosystem's, an entire ecosystem's, or a country's experience of equality, wellbeing, nonviolence, love and sustainability in all aspects of their life and situation

Environmental precautionary principle - called upon to challenge high power groups about their actions or plans where to act could cause irreparable harm to an individual part of an ecosystem, an entire ecosystem or country

Environmental sustainability – the ability to create a social system of production and exchange of goods and services that is not based on the exploitation of the natural world and its resources

Environmental rights – the obligation of individuals, groups and societies to uphold the intrinsic value of the natural world and not only because of its economic value to humans

Equal intrinsic worth – the belief that all sentient beings, non-sentient beings and nature-created materiality of the planet have worth by virtue of their existence. Human-made material entities and objects also have a value but not a higher value to nature as life creating

Equality - the experience of being free of discrimination and disadvantage. Fairness and recognition of the rights of humans, animals and the environment to live and flourish - see sustainability, ecojustice, love, nonviolence

Ethic of domination – the exercise of authoritarian and discriminatory influence over low power individuals and groups, creating an absence of nonviolence, love and ecojustice – see violence, discrimination, stigma (social), lovelessness

Ethic of love - the commitment to and practising of the love ethic, drawing on the eco-values of nonviolence, love and ecojustice – see love, love ethic work, love ethic model

Ethical use of self – the conscious and purposeful enacting of eco-values and love ethic informed ideas. It includes self-reflective and self-correcting actions to maintain personal and professional integrity - see professional integrity, professionalism, love ethic work, revolutionary, revolutionary practice

Ethical theories – sets of ideas and values which explicitly identify their ethical premises and implications for practice. Range from de-ontological, consequentialism, virtues, care-based to anti-oppressive theories including, Indigenous, posthumanism, veganism, feminism, and love ethic – see love ethic informed interpretations in the book title as follows – *The Revolutionary Social Worker: Love Ethic Companion*

Ethico-legal principles – significant moral claims that are located in, or implied by, legislation which influence how practitioners exercise their authority. Typically referred to as their duty to uphold these principles – see all principles commencing with 'duty of' or 'duty to' and love ethic informed interpretations in the book title as follows – *The Revolutionary Social Worker: Love Ethic Companion*

Ethics - the way individuals or groups enact their values in relationships and situations – see professional integrity, ethical use of self, love ethic work, love ethic informed, revolutionary practice, anti-oppressive practice

Exploitation – the unfair advantage gained at the expense of the low power individual, group or country – see cultural imperialism, privilege, racism, eco-injustice, oppression, violence

Feminism – a range of ideas typically developed by women from lived experience which articulate the harm caused by sexist oppression, how to address it and ways women can become empowered. Also seeks to contribute to other forms of oppression – see ecofeminism

Group – members of social or species groups, and aspects of ecosystems – e.g. forests, rivers, mountains

Group-based strategies – the strategic use of group processes with low power individuals and groups to empower and enable collective efforts to achieve ecojustice – see study circles, communities of practice, dialogical communities of practice

Harm – unwelcome intrusions against individuals' and groups' rights, wellbeing, bodily autonomy, cultural practices, sustainability and sovereignty – see unsafety, trauma, violence, lovelessness, eco-injustice

Healing – when love ethic informed actions or change is experienced by individuals, groups, communities or ecosystems as some combination of nonviolence, love and ecojustice relevant to the situation – see transformation, trauma informed care, empowerment, trauma informed organisations

High power individual or group - dominant or majority status and in specific situations, relatively greater access to power or resources – in relationship with low power individual or group

Human-centrism – the belief that human beings are superior to nonhuman animals and the environment, and therefore able to dominate or use other life forms - see anthropocentric harm, speciesism, oppression

Human rights – the upholding of the intrinsic equal worth of all people and thereby ensuring that all people are able to meet their needs and aspirations, provided no harm is caused to other people, animals or the environment

Inclusion – actions that uphold the safety, interests and equal intrinsic worth of individuals and groups – see safety, equal intrinsic worth, love ethic work

Inclusive governance – systems of socially sanctioned decision-making and related processes, often in the form of organisations, governments and businesses, that include the voices of low power individuals and groups – see voice, active participation, responsibility

Indigenous ethical theories – the diversity of First Nation Peoples' beliefs and ideas, in particular the ideas of ecology of being and the law being in the land and not in humans – see stewardship, equal intrinsic worth, posthumanism, postcolonialism

Individual – refers to and is inclusive of humans, animals and nature, unless otherwise explicitly stated

Inequality – discrimination creates or exacerbates inequality through personal, cultural and structural relationships of power

Injustice – see oppression

I-It relationship – the oppressive use of power by the dominant 'I' against an individual who is devalued and is treated as an object or as an 'It'

Interpersonal violence – all forms of harm enacted or threatened by individuals against other individuals, including childhood sexual abuse, domestic violence, workplace bullying, professional privilege (e.g. coercion of service users), abuse or killing of nonhuman animals, degradation of nature

Intersectionality – the interlinked compounding impacts of two or more types of oppression such that the individual or group has to negotiate greater levels of discrimination, stigma and harm

Intersectionality violence – the experience of violence which can be understood in terms of two or more social characteristics that are devalued by the high power individual or group

Intersubjectivity – individual and group identity and valuing is socially created and mediated, thus stigma and discrimination can impact the individual's and group's sense of worth and wellbeing

I-You relationship – reciprocal and loving interactions between two individuals who afford each other equal intrinsic worth

Justice – the diversity of nonviolent and loving actions which comprise movements towards and the substantive experience of fairness and love – see nonviolence, love, ecojustice

Land rights – First Nation Peoples' claims of sovereignty over their land in settler societies

Love – the diversity of actions that contribute to individual and group peace, care, wellbeing, justice, stewardship and sustainability – see nonviolence, ecojustice

Lovelessness – the denial of an individual or group with hate, homicidal, genocidal and ecocidal actions. Can also involve the undermining of expressions of love in a relationship with an individual or group by the use of violence

Love ethic – see ethic of love

Love ethic model – an adaptable set of values, strategies and processes for enabling loving, anti-oppressive practice with individuals and groups - see ethic of love, love ethic work, revolutionary practice

Love ethic work – the actions involved in enabling love ethic informed practice which includes, for example, Banks' (2016) emotion work, identity work and performance work

Love ethic informed – actions which consciously draw upon and accurately interpret the love ethic in relation to conventional ideas and practices

Low power individual or group – non-dominant or minority status and in specific situations, relatively less access to power and resources, compared with high power individuals or groups

Managerialism – an authoritarian system of governance in an organisation, where dominant ideas and processes are located in hierarchical and controlling relationships with front line staff. Directives can be out of step with the practitioner's obligations to act in the service users' interests – see moral unsafety, organisational violence, lovelessness, ethic of domination

Marginalisation – actions or failures of actions which cause an individual or group to be excluded, silenced, and denied justice claims

Minority group standpoint theory – any theory or idea which is based on lived experiences of low power individuals and groups which challenge and seek to change relevant dominant ideas and practices that cause them harm – see, for example, First Nation Peoples' ideas on racism and colonialism, feminism on sexist oppression

Moral injury – the lack of congruence between an individual's or group's values and how they are required, or able, to act

Moral safety – the experience of congruence between an individual's or group's values and how they are required, or able, to act

Movements – individual or collective actions that are love ethic informed in their relationships, processes and goals

Nature – the totality of life on the planet, the interconnectedness, reciprocity, renewal and death cycles where humans, nonhuman animals, landscapes and seascapes have agency and make a contribution to life

Natural justice (or procedural justice) – the non-discriminatory exercise of authority including fair actions, processes and decisions in relation to an individual or group

Nonviolence – the conscious cultivation of no harm and no retaliation by adopting the eco-values and following relevant aspects of the love ethic model – see love, ecojustice, non-maleficience

Non-maleficience – principle of doing no harm based on love informed ethic work – see nonviolence

Oppression – synonymous with injustice experienced by minority social groups, extended to include animal and environmental oppression. Includes powerlessness, violence, cultural imperialism, marginalisation, exploitation (Young, 1990), lovelessness and eco-injustice (including speciesism)

Organisational violence – the compounding and often hidden impact of interpersonal violence in organisational settings such as schools and universities, workplaces, businesses and government - see trauma organised workplaces, managerialism

Parallel process – mirroring of experiences such as trauma that can occur between practitioners and service users, albeit it different in nature for each group and in the power dynamics involved

Peace – the experience of nonviolence, love and ecojustice – see sustainability, equality

Physical safety - experiences of being able to maintain bodily autonomy and freedom of movement and not be subjected to any actions or failures to act that cause or threaten unwelcome impact on individuals' or groups' life, wellbeing and health

Pivoting – moving from a situation of violence, lovelessness or eco-injustice by turning on the energy of that issue with its opposite expression – see healing, transformation, transformational change leadership, love

Planetary pivoting – the collective flow on effects of individual and group pivoting – see healing, transformation, revolutionary, revolutionary practice

Positionality – the ability to be critically self reflective regarding how own power and status is used, to ensure no harm is caused and own actions align with loving, anti-oppressive ethics

Postcolonialism – the experience of justice and wellbeing for First

Nation People as a result of decolonisation

Posthumanism – a group of theories which argue for the equal intrinsic worth of humans, nonhuman animals, non-sentient entities as well as the spiritual and material dimensions of nature. Their respective rights to exist, without exploitation and their agency, intelligence and interconnectedness is recognised

Power (harmful) – the ability to influence individuals and groups where the range of mechanisms of power includes physical force, torture, threats of harm, coercion arising from failures to enact least restrictive practices, dominant discourses which stigmatise and blame low power individuals and groups

Power (loving) - the ability to influence individuals and groups using a range of love ethic informed power. Includes enabling, healing, transformation, being nonviolent, showing love, upholding ecojustice, non co-operation, resistance and challenging oppression

Powerlessness – the inability of the individual, group or country to act on their own understanding of what is in their best interests, and at a minimum the inability to protect themselves from unwelcome intrusions against their autonomy

Power-sensitive - being aware of the power dynamics – interpersonal, organisational, cultural and structural - and being responsive to its influence when engaging with an individual or group

Privilege – unearned or unfair advantage that is linked to harm of other individuals or groups. Privilege can also be used to address harm and 'pay forward' the gains from being privileged

Problematics of violence – evidence-based and analytical accounts of the nature of violence – interpersonal (including interspecies), organisational and intersectional – see violence, harm, trauma

Professional integrity – inclusive of personal integrity, where there is a conscious and purposeful commitment to aligning values and actions for nonviolence, love and ecojustice goals relevant to any specific situation

Professional privilege – the use of professional authority, status or resources to own advantage at the expense of individuals' or groups' interests and rights

Professionalism – the ability to act with integrity in work situations, see professional integrity, ethical use of self, love ethic work

Psychological safety – experiences of being affirmed and recognised that are congruent with own self or group awareness and self or group identity

Public interest – the highest expression possible of nonviolence, love and ecojustice, including the greatest protection possible of human, animal and environmental rights – see social, species and environmental precautionary principles

Reconciliation – the healing process undertaken by dominant individuals or groups to take responsibility for harm caused and to seek a nonviolent, loving and ecojust way forward, with the harmed individual or group

Relational ecology - humans are in relationships that are more than human, including with animals and are always within and part of nature

Relationship – the ability to interact in a meaningful way with another individual or group. The nature of being, ontology, is relational, and interlinks with reality as being socially constructed

Relationship-sensitive - being aware of the direct and indirect relationships, how these are infused with power and identity claims and, as well being context-sensitive, and being responsive to relational influences when engaging with an individual or group

Resistance – any nonviolent action that refuses to accept violence, lovelessness and injustice

Resisting with love – bringing a loving regard in the resistance action or work, for all parties

Responsibility – the ability to respond - see responsibility (for addressing harm) and responsibility (for raising ecojustice concerns)

Responsibility (for addressing harm) – the individual or group taking the proper order of accountability for hurting others and addressing the harm with substantive measures – see active participation, substantive measures, willingness to learn, willingness to love

Responsibility (for raising ecojustice concerns) – all citizens, including the impacted parties or their representatives raising ecojustice concerns – see active participation, voice

Retaliatory - see backlash

Revolutionary – a social worker, citizen (inclusive of asylum seekers and other non-citizens) or animal who lives according to, or in congruent ways with, the love ethic. Nature is already revolutionary due to their capacity to create and sustain life

Revolutionary practice – individuals' or groups' adoption of the love ethic and the love ethic model in work, home and public settings and the environment

Safety – the experience of psychological, physical, social and moral safety (Bloom 2017) - see nonviolence

Situated ethics – recognition that ethics are more than abstract ideas and need to be enacted in specific relationships and situations – see relationship-sensitive, context-sensitive, power-sensitive

Social action – group-based or collective nonviolent activism to address nonviolence, lovelessness and eco-injustice – see dialogical praxis, love ethic work, revolutionary practice

Social justice – the human individual, group or community level experience of equality, wellbeing, nonviolence, love and sustainability in all aspects of their life and situation

Social precautionary principle - high power groups challenged about their actions or plans where to act could cause irreparable harm to individuals, group of people or communities

Social safety - experiences of being affirmed and recognised in the range of social relationships including personal, work, community, interspecies and with nature

Social sustainability – a social system of relationships that is fair and respects and protects human rights and diversity, and disallows violence, lovelessness and eco-injustice

Social work – members of the social work profession, and individuals who uphold, or act in congruent ways with, the love ethic and related eco-values

Sociological imagination - the ability to think and envision which holds an awareness of the intersectionality between individual experiences and broader social, economic, cultural and historical influences

Species justice - the nonhuman individual and group level experience of equality, wellbeing, nonviolence, love and sustainability in all aspects of their life and situation

Species precautionary principle – high power groups challenged about their actions or plans where to act could cause irreparable harm to an individual or group of animals

Speciesism – an aspect of anthropocentrism where nonhuman animals are not treated with equal intrinsic worth and some animals are used, abused or killed for human benefit – see anthropocentrism, anthropocentric harm, violence

Stewardship – the loving of and caring for nonhuman individuals and groups and their interrelationships, including with humans

Stigma – individual stigma is where negative social judgements are internalised as shame; social stigma refers to the socio-cultural practices that perpetuate discrimination through shaming and stereotyping – see discrimination, disadvantage, violence, harm

Study circles – purposeful groups to build trust and capacity among the members to learn about the justice concern and prepare for social action - see group-based strategies, social action, empowerment

Substantive measures – the experience of ecojustice by the individuals, groups and ecosystems who are harmed, includes material gains, meeting of needs and other just improvements in quality of life

Sustainability – the experience of economic, social and environmental sustainability – see economic sustainability, social sustainability, environmental sustainability, ecojustice

Transformation – substantive change and healing by love for loving outcomes - see pivoting, planetary pivoting, movements, empowerment, healing, revolutionary practice

Transformational change leadership – an egalitarian, collaborative, love ethic informed approach to leadership. Can refer to the transformational change leader as an individual within the leadership team

Trauma – the impact of violence, harm and unsafety on and between individuals and groups

Trauma informed care – responding to an individual or group with a conscious commitment to avoid causing harm, to respectfully understand their experiences of trauma and to act in partnership to enable healing, wellbeing and justice

Trauma informed organisations – proactively designed and managed workplaces, particularly human service organisations, to ensure staff and service users are not harmed and where harm has occurred that this is addressed to avoid re-enactments of trauma

Trauma organised workplaces – the failure to design and manage human service organisations to be trauma informed, where harm is not addressed, compounds and perpetuates toxic and violent workplace cultures - see organisational violence, interpersonal violence, oppression

Unsafety – experiences of harm arising from intrusions against individuals' or groups' physical, psychological, social and moral safety – see harm, violence, discrimination, oppression

Values – cherished beliefs that the individual and group profess to uphold

Veganism – practising no harm and non-use of animals, being present (in love) with animals, recognising their agency and equal moral worth

Violence – the experience of harm, lovelessness or unsafety based on the perceived, threatened or enacted use of force against individuals, groups, communities and ecosystems – see oppression, discrimination, problematics of violence, interpersonal violence, organisational violence and intersectionality violence, lovelessness, eco-injustice

Voice – the expressed views and needs of individuals or groups, the right to have a voice and for this voice to be able to influence matters of concern to them. The recognition that voice includes a diversity of language and ways of being and communicating

Willingness to learn – integral to transformation and pivoting from lovelessness to love, involves being open to being influenced by other parties in the justice issue, relationship or situation

Willingness to love – feeling safe and empowered to love, including in situations of threat, challenge and injustice - see willingness to learn

References

_____

Abuelaish, I. (2012). *I shall not hate.* Bloomsbury Publishing.

Ainge Roy, E. (2017). *New Zealand river granted same legal rights as human being.* https://www.theguardian.com/world/2017/mar/16/new-zealand-river-granted-same-legal-rights-as-human-being

Animals Australia (2019). *5 easy ways to change the world for animals.* https://www.animalsaustralia.org/features/be-the-change-kind-2020.php

Anonymous for the Voiceless (2019). *Cube of truth.* https://www.anonymousforthevoiceless.org/what-is-a-cube-of-truth

Attorney-General's Department (2017a). *Final report. Our inquiry. Royal Commission into the Institutionalised Responses of Childhood Sexual Assault.* https://www.childabuseroyalcommission.gov.au/sites/default/files/final_report_-_volume_1_our_inquiry.pdf

Attorney-General's Department (2017b). *Narratives. Private sessions. Royal Commission into the Institutionalised Responses of Childhood Sexual Assault.* https://www.childabuseroyalcommission.gov.au/narratives?category=All&field_private_session_gender_value=All&field_state_value=All&field_decade_value=All&field_government_value=All&field_atsi_value=All&next=1

Australian Association of Social Workers, AASW (2010). *Code of ethics.* https://www.aasw.asn.au/practitioner-resources/code-of-ethics

Australian Council of Social Services (2018). *2018 poverty in Australia.* https://www.acoss.org.au/poverty/.

Australia's National Research Organisation for Women's Safety, ANROWS (2015). *Landscapes. State of knowledge.* https://apo.org.au/sites/default/files/resource-files/2015/10/apo-nid60675-1228771.pdf

Baines, D. (2016). Moral projects and compromise resistance: Resisting uncaring in nonprofit care work. *Studies in Political Economy, 97*(2), 124-142.

Baird, K. (2015). Women's lived experiences of domestic violence during pregnancy. *The Practising Midwife, 18,* 27-31.

Bakshi, R. (2013). Empathy and transformation: The search for well-being and justice after Gandhi. In J. Sethia & A. Narayan (Eds.), *The living Gandhi: Lessons for our times* (pp. 241-255). Penguin Books.

Banks, S. (2012). *Ethics and values in social work.* Palgrave Macmillan.

Banks, S. (2016). Everyday ethics in professional life: Social work as ethics work. *Ethics and Social Welfare, 10*(1), 35-52.

Banks, S., & Gallagher, A. (2009). *Ethics in professional life: Virtues for health and social care.* Palgrave Macmillan.

Barsky, A. (2017). *Conflict resolution for the helping professions* (3rd ed.). Thomson.

Barsky, A. (2019). *Ethics and values in social work* (2nd ed.). Oxford University Press.

Baum, F. (2018). *The new public health.* Oxford University Press.

Bates, M. (2014). *The emotional lives of dairy cows.* https://www.wired.com/2014/06/the-emotional-lives-of-dairy-cows/

Beauchamp, T, & Childress, F. (1985/2013). *Principles of biomedical ethics* (7th ed.). Oxford University Press.

Bennett, B. (2019). The importance of Aboriginal history for practitioners. In B. Bennett & S. Green (Eds.), *Our voices: Aboriginal social work* (2nd ed., pp. 3-30). Red Globe Press.

Bennett, B., Green, S., Gilbert, S., & Bessarab, D. (2013). *Our voices: Aboriginal and Torres Strait Islander social work* (1st ed.). Palgrave Macmillan.

Bennett, B., & Green, S. (2019). *Our voices: Aboriginal social work* (2nd ed.). Red Globe Press.

Berger, P., & Luckmann, T. (1967). *The social construction of reality.* Penguin Books.

Berry, D., & Pennebaker, J. (1993). Nonverbal and verbal emotional expression and health. *Psychotherapy and Psychosomatics, 59*(1), 11-19.

Bhabha, H. (1994). *The location of culture.* Routledge.

Bice, S., Brueckner, M., & Pforr, C. (2017). Putting social license to operate on the map: A social, actuarial and political risk and licensing model (SAP Model). *Resources Policy, 53*, 46-55.

Bloom, S. (2013). *Creating sanctuary: Toward the evolution of sane societies.* Routledge.

Bloom, S. (2017). *The sanctuary model: Through the lens of moral safety.* http://www.sanctuaryweb.com/Portals/0/Bloom%20 Pubs/2017%20Bloom%20Sanctuary%20Moral%20APA%20 Handbook.pdf

Bloom, S., & Farragher, B. (2010). *Destroying sanctuary: The crisis in human service delivery systems.* Oxford University Press.

Bloom, S., & Farragher, B. (2013). *Restoring sanctuary: A new operating system for trauma-informed systems of care.* Oxford University Press.

Bloom, S., & Reichert, M. (2014). *Bearing witness: Violence and collective responsibility.* Taylor and Francis.

Boetto, H. (2019). Advancing transformative eco-social change: Shifting from modernist to holistic foundations. *Australian Social Work, 72*(2), 139-152.

Boochani, B. (2018). *No friend but the mountains.* Picador.

Brady, D. (2020). Say no to Roe 8. In D. Ross, M. Brueckner, M. Palmer and W. Eaglehawk (Eds.), *Eco-activism and social work: New directions in leadership and group work* (pp. 74-88). Routledge.

Braidotti, R. (2013). *The posthuman.* Polity Press.

Braidotti, R. (2018). A theoretical framework for the critical posthumanities. *Theory, Culture and Society, 0*(0), 1-13.

Brophy, M. (2001). *The study circle: Participatory action research with and for the unemployed.* http://vuir.vu.edu.au/211/2/brophy.pdf.

Brubaker, M., Garrett, M., Rivera, E., & Tate, K. (2011). Justice making in groups for homeless adults: The emancipatory communitarianism way. In A. Singh & C. Salazaar (Eds.), *Social justice in group work* (pp. 34-43). Routledge.

Brueckner, M., & Ross, D. (2010). *Under corporate skies: A struggle between people, place and profit.* Fremantle Press.

Brueckner, M., & Ross, D. (2020). Eco-activism and social work: In the public interest. In D. Ross, M. Brueckner, M. Palmer & W. Eaglehawk (Eds.), *Eco-activism & social work: New directions in leadership and group work* (pp. 3-25). Routledge.

Bryant, W., & Bricknall, S. *(2017). Homicide in Australia 2012-2014: National homicide monitoring program report.* https://bit.ly/2ozctxh

Bryce, Q. (2015). *Not now, not ever report.* https://www.csyw.qld.gov.au/campaign/end-domestic-family-violence/about/not-now-not-ever-report

Buber, M. (1970). *I and Thou.* (trans. W. Kaufmann). Simon & Schuster.

Burbank, M. (2014). Prisons without bars and hospitals with locked doors. *Social Alternatives, 33*(3), 10-14.

Butot, M. (2004). *Love as emancipatory praxis.* https://dspace.library.uvic.ca/bitstream/handle/1828/402/butot_2004.pdf?sequence=1&isAllowed=y

Bykova, M. (2016). New insights into Aristotle's ethics. *Russian Studies in Philosophy, 54*(6), 449–455.

Canadian Counselling and Psychotherapy Association (2007). *Code of ethics.* https://www.ccpa-accp.ca/wp-content/uploads/2014/10/CodeofEthics_en.pdf

Chavulak, J., & Petrakis, M. (2017). Who experiences seclusion? *Social Work Health Care*, *56*(6), 524-540.

Chenoweth, E., & Stephan, M. (2011). *Why civil resistance works: The strategic logic of nonviolent conflict*. Columbia University Press.

Chokr, N. (2004). *Foucault on power and resistance: Another take – toward a post-postmodern political philosophy*. https://www.researchgate.net/publication/314235186_Foucault_on_Power_and_Resistance_Another_Take_--Toward_a_Post-postmodern_Political_Philosophy

Clark, K., Barnes, M., & Ross, D. (2018). 'I had no other option': Women, ECT and informed consent. *Journal of Mental Health Nursing*, 27, 1077-1085.

Cleary, P. (2012). *Mine-field: The dark side of Australia's resources rush*. Black Inc.

Cleary, P. (2017). Title fight: The great philanthropist vs the people of the Pilbara. *The Monthly* (pp. 24-32). https://www.themonthly.com.au/

Conflict Resolution Network (2019). *Resolve the conflict guide.* https://www.crnhq.org/resolve-the-conflict-guide/

D'Aunno, L., & Heinz, M. (2017). *Continuing courageous conversations toolkit.* http://www.polkdecat.com/Toolkit%20for%20Courageous%20Conversations.pdf

Denzin, N. (1997). *Interpretive ethnography: Ethnographic practices for the 21st century.* Sage Publications.

Dobash, R., & Dobash, R. (1979). *Violence against wives: A case against the patriarchy.* Free Press.

DV Connect (2019). *What is domestic violence?* http://www.dvconnect.org/womensline/what-is-domestic-violence/

Eaglehawk, W. (2020). Species justice is for every body. In D. Ross, M. Brueckner, M. Palmer & W. Eaglehawk (Eds.), *Eco-activism and social work: New directions in leadership and group work* (pp. 100-110). Routledge.

Ellis, C., & Flaherty, M. (Eds). (1992). *Investigating subjectivity: Research on lived experience.* Sage Publications.

Eswaran, V. (2018). *Vegetarianism is good for the economy too.* https://www.weforum.org/agenda/2018/12/vegetarian-ism-is-good-for-the-economy-too/

Fine, A. (Ed.). (2019). *Handbook on animal-assisted therapy: Theoretical foundations and guidelines for animal-assisted interventions* (5th ed.). Academic Press.

Fitz-Gibbon, K. & Maher, J. (2018). *Men's violence against women: The leading threat to women's safety and wellbeing.* https://lens.monash.edu/2018/10/17/1362647/the-number-one-threat-to-womens-safety-and-well-being

Fook, J. (2016). *Social work: A critical approach to practice.* Sage.

Fox, K. (2018). *Here's why you should turn your business vegan in 2018.* https://www.forbes.com/sites/katrinafox/2017/12/27/heres-why-you-should-turn-your-business-vegan-in-2018/#69a32612144d

Fox, C., & Miller, H. (1995). *Postmodern public administration: Towards discourse.* Sage Publications.

Francione, G. (2016). *Veganism as a moral imperative.* https://www.abolitionistapproach.com/veganism-moral-imperative/

Francione, G., & Charlton, A. (2013). *Animal rights: The abolitionist approach.* Exempla Press.

Fraser, N. (2009). Who counts? Dilemmas of justice in a post west-phalian world. *Antipode, 41*(1), 281-297.

Freire, P. (1970). *Pedagogy of the oppressed.* Penguin Books.

Furtak, R. (2018). Emotional knowing: The role of embodied feelings in affective cognition. *Philosophia, 46,* 575–587.

Gaard, G. (2011). Ecofeminism revisited: Rejecting essentialism and re-placing species in a material feminist environmentalism. *Feminist Formulations, 23,* 26-53.

Gandhi, R. (2013). Gandhi's journey to ahimsa. In J. Sethia & A. Narayan (Eds.), *The living Gandhi: Lessons for our times* (pp. 101-117). Penguin Books.

Godden, N. (2016). A co-operative inquiry about love using narrative, performative and visual methods. *Qualitative Research, 17*(1), 3-19.

Godden, N. (2017). The love ethic: A radical theory for social work practice. *Australian Social Work, 70*(4), 405-416.

Godden, N. (2018). Love in community work in rural Timor-Leste: A co-operative inquiry for a participatory framework for practice. *Community Development Journal, 53*(1), 78-98.

Gray, M. (2009). Moral sources and emergent ethical theories in social work. *British Journal of Social Work, 40*, 1794-1811.

Green, S. (2018). Aboriginal People and caring within a colonised society. In B. Pease, A. Vreugdenhil and S. Stanford (Eds.), *Critical ethics of care in social work: Transforming the politics and practices of caring* (pp. 139-147). Routledge.

Green, S., Bennett, B., Collins, A., Gowans, B., Hennessey, K., & Smith, K. (2013). Walking the journey: The student experience. In B. Bennett & S. Green (Eds.). *Our voices: Aboriginal social work* (2nd ed.). (pp. 3-30). Red Globe Press.

Hanh, T.N. (1991). *Peace is every step: The path of mindfulness in everyday life.* Bantam Books.

Haraway, D. (2015). Anthropocene, Capitalocene, Planationocene, Chthulucene: Making kin. *Environmental Humanities, 6*, 159-165.

Harvey, J. (2016). *Indigenous business has plenty to teach about values-led business.* https://www.theguardian.com/ sustainable-business/2016/nov/29/indigenous-business-has-plenty-to-teach-about-values-led-business

Hem, M., Gjerberg, E., Husum, T., & Pedersen, R. (2018). Ethical challenges when using coercion in mental health are: A systematic review. *Nursing Ethics, 25*(1), 92-110.

Hirst, R., Moginie, J., Garrett, P., Rotsey, M., & Stevens, W. (1990). *Blue sky mine.* [Midnight Oil].

hooks, b. (1994). *Outlaw culture: Resisting representations.* Routledge.

hooks, b. (2000a). *All about love.* New Visions.

hooks, b. (2000b). *Feminism is for everybody.* Pluto Press.

hooks, b. (2001). *Salvation: Black people and love.* William Morrow.

hooks, b. (2008). *Belonging: A culture of place.* Routledge.

Howard, C. (2007). Three models of individualised biography. In C. Howard (Ed.). *Contested individualisation* (pp. 25-43). Macmillan.

Hughes, M. (2018). Where is the love? Meditations on a critical ethic of care and love in social work. In B. Pease, A. Vreugdenhil & S. Stanford (Eds.), *Critical ethics of care in social work: Transforming the politics and practices of caring* (pp. 197-206). Routledge.

Hyde, C. (2018). Leading from below: Low power actors as organisational change agents. *Human Service Organisations: Management, Leadership & Governance, 42*(1), 53-67.

International Federation of Social Workers (2018). *Global social work statement of ethical principles. https://www.ifsw.org/global-social-work-statement-of-ethical-principles/*

Intergovernmental Science-Policy Platform on Biodiversity and Ecosystem Services (2019). *UN report: Nature's dangerous decline 'unprecedented': Species extinction rates 'accelerating'.* https://www.un.org/sustainabledevelopment/blog/2019/05/nature-decline-unprecedented-report/

Isay, D. (2016). *Listening as an act of love.* https://onbeing.org/programs/david-isay-listening-as-an-act-of-love/

Jecks, D. (2020). Hands off Point Peron. In D. Ross, M. Brueckner, M. Palmer and W. Eaglehawk (Eds.). *Eco-activism and social work: New directions in leadership and group work* (pp. 89-99). Routledge.

Kaushik, A. (2017). Use of self in social work: Rhetoric or reality? *Journal of Social Work Values and Ethics, 14*(1), 21-29.

Kelly, A., & Westoby, P. (2018). *Participatory development practice: Using traditional and contemporary frameworks.* Practical Action Publishing.

Khoury, S., & Whyte, D. (2017). *How human rights law has been used to guarantee corporations a 'right to profit'.* http://theconversation.com/how-human-rights-law-has-been-used-to-guarantee-corporations-a-right-to-profit-74593

King, M. (1999). *Mahatma Gandhi and Martin Luther King Jr.: The power of nonviolent action.* UNESCO Publishing.

King, M. L. (1957). *Loving your enemies.* http://okra.stanford.edu/transcription/document_images/Vol04S-cans/315_17-Nov-1957_Loving%20Your%20Enemies.pdf

Lather, P., & Smithies, C. (1997). *Troubling the angels: Women living with HIV/AIDS.* Westview Press.

Leonard, P. (1997). *Postmodern welfare: Reconstructing an emancipatory project.* Sage.

Levitt, T. (2018). *Dairy's 'dirty secret': It's still cheaper to kill male calves than to rear them.* https://www.theguardian.com/environment/2018/mar/26/dairy-dirty-secret-its-still-cheaper-to-kill-male-calves-than-to-rear-them

Lim, E., Wynaden, D., & Heslop, K. (2018). Changing practice using recovery-focused care in acute mental health settings to reduce aggression: A qualitative study. *International Journal of Mental Health Nursing,* doi/epdf/10.1111/inm.12524

Lorde, A. (1979/2018). *The master's tools will never dismantle the master's house.* Penguin Modern.

Lukes, S. (1974). *Power: A radical view.* Macmillan.

Macy, J. (2019). *Joanna Macy and her work.* https://www.joannamacy.net/main

Mandela, N. (2013). *Long walk to freedom.* Hachette Digital.

Martin, K. (2003). *Ways of knowing, being and doing: A theoretical framework and methods for Indigenous and Indigenist.* http://www.api-network.com/main/pdf/scholars/jas76_martin.pdf

Matsumoto, K. (2018). *Face is everything in Japan.* https://talkaboutja-pan.com/save-face-in-japanese-culture/

McAuliffe, D. (2014). *Interprofessional ethics: Collaboration in the social, health & human services.* Cambridge University Press.

McDonald, A. (2011). *Teens who smoke pot at risk for later schizo-phrenia, psychosis.* https://www.health.harvard.edu/blog/teens-who-smoke-pot-at-risk-for-later-schizophrenia-psychosis-201103071676

Meyer, I., Forkman, B., & Paul, E. (2015). Factors affecting the human interpretation of dog behaviour. *Anthrzoos*, 127-140.

Mies, M., & Shiva, V. (1993). *Ecofeminism*. Zed Books.

Mills, C. (1953). *The power elite*. Oxford University Press.

Mills, C. (1959). *The sociological imagination*. Oxford University Press.

Moore, J. (2016). The rise of cheap nature. In J. Moore (Ed.). *Anthropocene or Capitalocene? Nature, history, and the crisis of capitalism* (pp. 78-116). PM Press.

Morgan, A. (2000). *What is narrative therapy? An easy to read introduction*. https://dulwichcentre.com.au/what-is-narrative-therapy/

Moro, A. (2016). Understanding the dynamics of violent political revolutions in an agent-based framework. *PLOS ONE 11*(4), 1-17.

Mullaly, B., & West, J. (2017). *Challenging oppression & confronting privilege* (3rd ed.). Oxford University Press.

Nagesh, A. (2017). *The harrowing psychological toll of slaughterhouse work*. https://metro.co.uk/2017/12/31/how-killing-animals-everyday-leaves-slaughterhouse-workers-traumatised-7175087/

National Mental Health Consumers and Carers Forum (2009). *Position statement*. http://www.nmhccf.org.au/documents/Seclusion%20&%20Restraint.pdf

Nicolaou, E., & Smith, C. (2019). *A #ME Too timeline to show how far we've come and how far we need to go*. https://www.refinery29.com/en-us/2018/10/212801/me-too-movement-history-timeline-year-weinstein

Nussbaum, M. (2013). *Political emotions: Why love matters for justice*. Belkaap Press.

Oliver, P. (2013). Critical mass theory. In D. Snow, D. della Porta & B. Klandrmans (Eds.), *The Wiley Blackwell encyclopedia of social and political movements*. https://doi.org/10.1002/9780470674871.wbespm059

Ortega, R. (2017). Group work and socially just practice. In C. Garvin, L. Gutierrez & M. Galinsky (Eds.), *Handbook of social work with groups* (2nd ed., pp. 93-110). The Guilford Press.

Our Consumer Place (2020). *Our consumer place resources*. http://www.ourconsumerplace.com.au/consumer/resources

Palmer, M. (2015). Wicked problems. In S. Idowu (Ed.), *International dictionary of corporate social responsibility* (pp. 578-579). Springer.

Palmer, M., & Ross, D. (2014). Tracing the maddening effects of abuses of authority: Rationalities gone violent in mental health services and universities. *Social Alternatives, 33*(3), 28-36.

Pease, B. (2010). *Undoing privilege: Unearned advantage in a divided world*. Zed Books.

Pease, B., Vreugdenhil, A., & Stanford, S. (Eds.). (2018). *Critical ethics of care in social work: Transforming the politics and practices of caring*. Routledge.

Peavey, F. (2000). *Heart politics revisited*. Pluto Press.

People for Ethical Treatment of Animals (PETA) (2019). *Can the greatness of a nation?* https://www.peta.org/features/gandhi/

People for Ethical Treatment of Animals (PETA) (2020). *Animals are not ours*. https://www.peta.org.au/

Perroni, E. (2019). *A regenerative era in Australian agriculture is emerging*. https://sustainablefoodtrust.org/articles/a-regenerative-era-in-australian-agriculture-is-emerging/

Plumwood, V. (1993). *Feminism and the mastery of nature*. Routledge.

Plumwood, V. (2000). Integrating ethical framework for animals, humans and nature: A critical feminist ecological-societal analysis. *Ethics and the Environment, 5*(2), 285-322.

Plumwood, V. (2002). *Environmental culture: The ecological crisis of reason*. Routledge.

Poelina, A. (2020). Foreward. First Law is the natural law of the land. In D. Ross, M. Brueckner, M. Palmer & W. Eaglehawk (Eds.), *Eco-activism & social work: New directions in leadership and group work* (pp. viii-xii). Routledge.

Reality Check Team BBC News (2020). *Australia fires: How do we know how many animals have died?* https://www.bbc.com/

news/50986293

Rogers, C. (1951). *Client-centred therapy: Its current practice, implications and theory.* Houghton & Miffin.

Ross, D. (2002). *Enacting my theory and politics of an ethic of love in social work education.* Edith Cowan University.

Ross, D. (2013). Social work and the struggle for corporate social responsibility. In M. Gray, J. Coates, & T. Hetherington (Eds.). *Environmental social work* (pp. 193-210). Routledge.

Ross, D. (2014). The wicked problem of violences in mad/places and people. *Social Alternatives, 33*(3), 3-9.

Ross, D. (2015). Social sustainability. In S. Idowu (Ed.), *Dictionary of corporate social responsibility* (p. 466). Springer.

Ross, D. (2017). A research-based model for corporate social responsibility: Towards accountability to impacted stakeholders. *Journal of Corporate Social Responsibility, 2*(8), 1-11.

Ross, D. (2019). Practising community and dialogical communities of practice for ecological justice and loving relationships. *Journal of Australian Community Work, 1,* 1-13.

Ross, D. (2020). The love ethic practice model. In D. Ross, M. Brueckner, M. Palmer & W. Eaglehawk (Eds.), *Eco-activism & social work: New directions in leadership and group work* (pp. 125-142). Routledge.

Ross, D., Bennett, B., & Menyweather, N. (forthcoming). Towards a critical posthumanist social work: Trans species ethics of ecological justice, nonviolence and love. In V. Bozalek and B. Pease (Eds.). *Post-anthropocentric social work: Critical posthumanism and new materialist perspectives.* Routledge.

Ross, D., Brueckner, M., Palmer, M., & Eaglehawk, W. (Eds.). (2020). *Eco-activism & social work: New directions in leadership and group work.* Routledge.

Ross, D., & Palmer, M. (2020). Transformational change leadership and dialogue between groups. In D. Ross, M. Brueckner, M. Palmer & W. Eaglehawk (Eds.), *Eco-activism & social work: New directions in leadership and group work* (pp. 143-162). Routledge.

Ross, D., & Puccio, V. (2020). Homegrown community activism in Yarloop. In D. Ross, M. Brueckner, M. Palmer & W. Eaglehawk (Eds.), *Eco-activism & social work: New directions in leadership and group work* (pp. 26-38). Routledge.

Ryan, T. (2011). *Animals and social work: A moral introduction.* Palgrave MacMillan.

Seidman, S. (2016). *Contested knowledge: Social theory today* (5th ed.). Wiley-Blackwell.

Seiver, H. (2020). Just(ice) arts in practice: Processes and collaborations. In D. Ross, M. Brueckner, M. Palmer and W. Eaglehawk (Eds.), *Eco-activism and social work: New directions in leadership and group work* (pp. 49-60). Routledge.

Sengupta, S. (2020). *Greta Thunberg's message at Davos forum: 'Our house is still on fire'.* https://www.nytimes.com/2020/01/21/climate/greta-thunberg-davos.html

Sentient Media (2019). *How many animals are killed for food every day?* https://sentientmedia.org/how-many-animals-are-killed-for-food-every-day/

Sharp, G. (2005). *Waging nonviolence struggle: 20th century practice and 21st century potential.* Extending Horizons Books.

Shier, M., Nicholas, D., Graham, J., & Young, A. (2018). Preventing workplace violence in human services workplaces. *Human Service Organisations: Management, Leadership & Governance, 42*(1), 4-18.

Shiva, V. (2014). *The Vandana Shiva reader.* University of Kentucky Press.

Simard, S. (2016). *How trees talk to each other.* https://www.youtube.com/watch?v=Un2yBgIAxYs

Singh, A., & Salazar, C. (Eds.). (2011). *Social justice in group work: Practical interventions for change.* Routledge.

Stanley, L., & Wise, S. (1983). *Breaking out: Feminist consciousness and feminist research.* Routledge.

Starhawk (1988). *Dreaming the dark: Magic, sex and politics.* Beacon Press.

Stevanovic, M., & Koski, S. (2018). Intersubjectivity and the domains of social interaction: Proposal of a cross-sectional approach. *Psychology of Language and Communication, 22*(1), 39-70.

Substance Abuse and Mental Health Services Administration (SAMSHA) (2015). *Trauma-informed approach and trauma-specific interventions.* http://www.samhsa.gov/nctic/trauma-interventions

Substance Abuse and Mental Health Services Administration (SAMSHA) (2018). *Roadmap to seclusion and restraint free mental health services.* https://www.samhsa.gov/trauma-violence/seclusion

Sutton, P. (2010). Aboriginal spirituality in a new age. *The Australian Journal of Anthropology, 21*(1), 71-89.

Suzuki, D. (1997). *The sacred balance: Rediscovering our place in nature.* Allen & Unwin.

Swedish Union for Social Sciences Professionals (2015). *Ethics in social work: A code of conduct and ethical behaviour for social workers.* https://akademssr.se/sites/default/files/files/ETHICS%20IN%20SOCIAL%20WORK%20w.pdf

Taylor, A. (2013). *Reconfiguring the natures of childhood.* Routledge.

Taylor, A., & Pacini-Kerchabaw, V. (2018). *The common worlds of children and animals: Relational ethics for entangled lives.* Routledge.

Thoit, P. (2016). "I'm not mentally ill": Identity deflection as a form of stigma resistance. *Journal of Health and Social Behaviour, 57*(2), 135-151.

Thompson, N. (2018). *Promoting equality: Working with diversity and difference.* Palgrave Macmillan.

Tingleff, E., Bradley, S., Gilbert, F., Munksgaard, G., & Houndsgaard, L. (2017). "Treat me with respect." A systematic review and thematic analysis of psychiatric patients' reported perceptions of the situations associated with the process of coercion. *Journal of Psychiatric and Mental Health Nursing, 24*, 681-698.

Tiruneh, G. (2014). *Social revolution: Their causes, patterns and phases.* https://doi.org/10.1177/2158244014548845

Tochkov, K., & Williams, N. (2018). Patient or prisoner? Forced treatment for the severely mentally ill. *Ethical Human Psychology and Psychiatry, 20*(1), 56-68.

Thomashow, M. (2014). *The ecological imagination: A portfolio of possibilities.* http://www.mitchellthomashow.com/ecological-imagination/2014/12/19/what-is-the-ecological-imagination

Ury, W. (2019). *The walk from no to yes.* https://www.ted.com/talks/william_ury_the_walk_from_no_to_yes/transcript?language=en

Valdiva, A. (2002). bell hooks: Ethics from the margins. *Qualitative Inquiry, 8*(4), 429-447.

Watts, J. (2015). *Gender, health and healthcare.* Ashgate.

Wenger, E., & Snyder, W. (2000). *Communities of practice: The organisational frontier.* https://hbr.org/2000/01/communities-of-practice-the-organizational-frontier

Willett, C. (2014). *Interspecies ethics.* Columbia University Press.

White, R. (2009). Environmental victims and resistance to state crime through transnational activism. *Social Justice, 36*(3), 46-60.

White, R. (2017). Corruption and the securitisation of nature. *International Journal for Crime, Justice and Social Democracy, 6*(4), 55-70.

White, R. (2018). Ecocentrism & criminal justice. *Theoretical Criminology, 22*(3), 342-362.

Woodley, M. (2020). The wrong side of Native title, the right side of mining. In D. Ross, M. Brueckner, M. Palmer and W. Eaglehawk (Eds.), *Eco-activism and social work: New directions in leadership and group work* (pp. 61-73). Routledge.

World Health Organisation WHO (2013). *Violence against women: A global health problem of epidemic proportions.* https://www.who.int/mediacentre/news/releases/2013/violence_against_women_20130620/en/

Young, I. (1990). *Justice and the politics of difference.* Princeton University Press.

www.ingramcontent.com/pod-product-compliance
Lightning Source LLC
Chambersburg PA
CBHW032150020426
42334CB00016B/1256